purity 365

DAILY REFLECTIONS ON TRUE LOVE

JASON EVERT

SERVANT
BOOKS

PUBLISHED BY ST. ANTHONY MESSENGER PRESS
CINCINNATI, OHIO

Unless otherwise noted, Scripture passages have been taken from the *Revised Standard Version*, Catholic edition. Copyright © 1946, 1952, 1971 by the Division of Christian Education of the National Council of Churches of Christ in the USA. Used by permission. All rights reserved. Scripture passages marked *NAB* have been taken from *New American Bible*, New York: Catholic Book, 1991. Note: The editors of this volume have made minor changes in capitalization to some of the Scripture quotations herein. Please consult the original source for proper capitalization. Quotations are taken from the English translation of the *Catechism of the Catholic Church* for the United States of America (indicated as CCC), 2nd ed. Copyright 1997 by United States Catholic Conference—Libreria Editrice Vaticana. Excerpts from *The Way*, by Josemaría Escrivá, ©2002, Studium Foundation, are used by permission of Scepter Publishers. Excerpts from *The Quotable Saint*, by Rosemary Ellen Guiley, copyright ©2002, Checkmark Books, an imprint of Infobase Publishing, are reprinted with permission of Checkmark Books.

Cover design by Saint Louis Creative/Devin Schadt
Cover image by Saint Louis Creative 2009
Book design by Mark Sullivan

LIBRARY OF CONGRESS CATALOGING-IN-PUBLICATION DATA
Evert, Jason.
Purity 365 : daily reflections on true love / Jason Evert.
p. cm.
Includes bibliographical references and index.
ISBN 978-0-86716-936-2 (pbk. : alk. paper) 1. Catholic teenagers—Religious life. 2. Catholic teenagers—Sexual behavior—Quotations, maxims, etc. 3. Love—Religious aspects—Catholic Church—Quotations, maxims, etc. 4. Devotional calendars. 5. Christian saints—Prayers and devotions. I. Title. II. Title: Purity three hundred sixty-five.
BX2355.E94 2009
242'.64—dc22
2009026563

ISBN 978-0-86716-936-2

Published by Servant Books, an imprint of St. Anthony Messenger Press.
28 W. Liberty St.
Cincinnati, OH 45202
www.ServantBooks.org

Printed in the United States of America.

Printed on acid-free paper.

09 10 11 12 13 5 4 3 2 1

CONTENTS

INTRODUCTION

Teenagers today are often discouraged by the concept of chastity, seeing it as nothing more than an invitation to avoid sexual intimacy for about a decade. Meanwhile, young adults might question the practicality of abstinence and wonder when a worthy spouse will enter their lives. In both cases modern singles sometimes question their morals and assume that they need to lower their standards in order to find love and acceptance. As a result of such frustration, many excuse themselves from the demands of pure love.

What these young adults do not realize is that they have defined purity as the absence of intimacy instead of what it really is: a virtue necessary for establishing the most intimate of all human loves. Not only does it train a person in faithfulness, Pope John Paul II explained that chastity frees a couple from a selfish attitude of using one another and makes them capable of authentic human love. Without an interior attitude of reverence and even awe toward the other person, human love is unable to become what it is meant to be: a reflection of the very love of God. This is why chastity is so essential even within marriage, as a reverent attitude toward the gift of sexuality.

Because the media saturates our culture with lust 365 days a year, a daily inoculation of purity is helpful—thus the purpose of this book. Within its pages you'll find daily quotes on true love from saints, teenagers, married people and others whose wisdom is tried and true. You'll notice that I have placed a heavy emphasis on some modern icons of holiness, such as Pope John Paul II, Blessed Mother Teresa of Calcutta and Saint Josemaría Escrivá.

In the preface to his spiritual classic *The Way*, Saint Josemaría Escrivá offers a piece of advice that I would echo to you as you prepare to read this book:

> Read these counsels slowly.
> Pause to meditate on these thoughts.
> They are things that I whisper in your ear—
> confiding them—
> as a friend, as a brother. . . .
>
> And they are being heard by God.
>
> I won't tell you anything new.
> I will only stir your memory,
> so that some thought will arise
> and strike you;
> and so you will better your life
> and set out along the ways of prayer
> and of love.

And in the end you will be
a more worthy soul.[1]

Beneath each day's quote you will find a saint whose feast is celebrated by the Catholic Church on that particular day. Some of their names you will recognize, such as Saints Peter, Joseph and Mary. Others you may never have seen before, such as Saints Ishyrion and Turibius de Mogrovejo. Several are teenagers, while others were martyred together as husband and wife.

Each has a fascinating story, such as Saint Vitalis of Gaza. He earned his money by doing manual labor and spent his wages on prostitutes. However, he did not sin with them. Instead he prayed with them through the night and taught them the gospel. He converted many, and he was eventually murdered by someone who did not understand his saintly motives.

Regardless of whether or not you have heard of the saints we invoke in this book, they all know of you. In the book of Revelation, we read of people in heaven who stand before the throne of God and offer to him our prayers as incense (see Revelation 5:8). Three chapters later we read of an angel interceding for us in the same way (Revelation 8:3). We know from the Bible that the fervent prayer of a righteous person is very powerful (James 5:16), and those in heaven have been perfected in righteousness. Therefore it is wise for us to seek their intercession.

Next to each saint's name is the phrase "pray for us." Do not merely read these lines. Pray them. Ask each specific saint to intercede for you to grow in the virtue of purity. As you do so, realize that they know your struggles. They all faced temptation and won. Some of them even lost their lives to preserve their purity.

By the end of the year, you will have asked nearly four hundred saints to remember you in their prayers as they stand before the unveiled glory of the Blessed Trinity. If you've ever felt alone in your efforts to lead a clean life, remember that you are always surrounded by this great cloud of witnesses (see Hebrews 12:1).

—*Jason Evert*
Feast of Saint Joseph the Worker, 2008

JANUARY

· · · · · · · · · · · · · ·

January 1

Devotion to the Blessed Sacrament and devotion to the Blessed Virgin are not simply the best way, but in fact the only way to keep purity. At the age of twenty nothing but Communion can keep one's heart pure.... Chastity is not possible without the Eucharist. —SAINT PHILIP NERI

Mary, Mother of God, pray for us.

· · · · · · · · · · · · · ·

January 2

There is dullness, monotony, sheer boredom in all of life when virginity and purity are no longer protected and prized. By trying to grab fulfillment everywhere, we find it nowhere. —ELISABETH ELLIOT

Saint Gregory Nazianzen, pray for us.

· · · · · · · · · · · · · ·

. . . .

January 3

[I]n proportion to our victories over these petty foes will be the number of jewels in that crown of glory which God makes ready for us in Paradise. —SAINT FRANCIS DE SALES

Saint Genevieve, pray for us.

. . . .

January 4

In seeking a soul mate,... it's helpful not to forget your own soul.—WENDY SHALIT

Saint Elizabeth Ann Seton, pray for us.

. . . .

January 5

Christ is found particularly in the field of sexual morality, because it is here that Christ makes demands on men. —POPE JOHN PAUL II

Saint John Neumann, pray for us.

. . . .

. . . .

January 6

Jesus tells us that the pure of heart will see God. That alone is enough for me. —MALE COLLEGE STUDENT

Blessed André Bessette, pray for us.

. . . .

January 7

The fingerprint of God on a relationship is purity and peace.—JASON EVERT

Saint Raymond of Peñafort, pray for us.

. . . .

January 8

So shun youthful passions and aim at righteousness, faith, love, and peace, along with those who call upon the Lord from a pure heart.—2 TIMOTHY 2:22

Saint Apollinaris, pray for us.

. . . .

. . . .

January 9

In your strife with the Devil, you have for spectators the angels and the Lord of angels. —SAINT EPHRAEM

Saint Adrian of Canterbury, pray for us.

. . . .

January 10

To be pure, to remain pure, can only come at a price, the price of knowing God and of loving him enough to do his will. He will always give us the strength we need to keep purity as something beautiful for God.
—BLESSED TERESA OF CALCUTTA

Saint William of Bourges, pray for us.

. . . .

January 11

The most powerful thing you can do on earth is the will of God.—CRYSTALINA EVERT

Saint Vitalis of Gaza, pray for us.

. . . .

· · · · · · · · · · · · ·

January 12

God desires the least degree of purity of conscience in you
more than all the works you can perform.
—SAINT JOHN OF THE CROSS

Saint Marguerite Bourgeoys, pray for us.

· · · · · · · · · · · · ·

January 13

The alternative is clear: either man governs his passions
and finds peace, or he lets himself be dominated by them
and becomes unhappy. —CATECHISM OF THE CATHOLIC CHURCH,
2339; SEE SIRACH 1:22

Saint Hilary of Poitiers, pray for us.

· · · · · · · · · · · · ·

January 14

There are few better tests for whether or not someone lives
a life in submission to God than what he or she does with
their sexuality. Sex is such a powerful and meaningful desire
that to give it up and obey God in that area is a true sign of
worship. —DRS. HENRY CLOUD AND JOHN TOWNSEND

Saint Sava, pray for us.

· · · · · · · · · · · · ·

. . . .

January 15
[I]t is the nature of our enemy to become powerless,
lose courage, and take to flight as soon as a person who
is following the spiritual life stands courageously against
his temptations and does exactly the opposite to
what he suggests. —SAINT IGNATIUS OF LOYOLA

Saint Ita, pray for us.

. . . .

January 16
He did not say: You will not be troubled—you will not be
tempted—you will not be distressed. But He said: "You will
not be overcome." —SAINT JULIAN OF NORWICH

Saint Marcellus, pray for us.

. . . .

January 17
A woman should be so hidden in Christ that a man has to
see Christ just to see her. —HIGH SCHOOL FEMALE

Saint Anthony the Abbot, pray for us.

. . . .

. . . .

January 18

No one becomes perfect at once; but as from little faults we fall into great, so by the practice of lesser virtues we ascend to the heroic. —VENERABLE CATHERINE MCAULEY

Saint Volusian, pray for us.

. . . .

January 19

[L]ove is not merely a feeling; it is an act of will that consists of preferring, in a constant manner, the good of others to the good of oneself. —POPE JOHN PAUL II

Saint Canute, pray for us.

. . . .

January 20

True love causes pain.
Jesus, in order to give us the proof of his love, died on the cross.
A mother, in order to give birth to her baby, has to suffer.
If you really love one another, you will not be able to avoid making sacrifices.

—BLESSED TERESA OF CALCUTTA

Saint Sebastian, pray for us.

. . . .

. . . .

January 21

He who loves purity of heart,
and whose speech is gracious, will have the king
as his friend. —PROVERBS 22:11

Saint Agnes, pray for us.

. . . .

January 22

I view my body as a shrine that only one man will ever see,
my husband. —HIGH SCHOOL FEMALE

Saint Vincent of Saragossa, pray for us.

. . . .

January 23

If you want to know the will of God as it relates to purity,
go to him in prayer. He's not waiting to take something
away from you. He's waiting to teach you to love.
—JASON EVERT

Saint Ildephonsus, pray for us.

. . . .

. . . .

January 24

Whatever temptations, then, assault you, and whatever attraction ensues, so long as your will refuses to consent to either, be not afraid, God is not displeased.

—SAINT FRANCIS DE SALES

Saint Francis de Sales, pray for us.

. . . .

January 25

No temptation has overtaken you that is not common to man. God is faithful, and he will not let you be tempted beyond your strength, but with the temptation will also provide the way of escape, that you may be able to endure it.

—1 CORINTHIANS 10:13

Saint Paul, pray for us.

. . . .

January 26

[E]very time I give in [to temptation], it wears down my resistance, but every time I resist, I grow stronger.

—DAWN EDEN

Saint Paula, pray for us.

. . . .

· · · · · · · · · · ·

January 27

Purity is beautiful. It crowns natural beauty with mystery.

—CRYSTALINA EVERT

Saint Angela Merici, pray for us.

· · · · · · · · · · ·

January 28

No man can live without delight, and that is why a man deprived of spiritual joy goes over to carnal pleasures.

—SAINT THOMAS AQUINAS

Saint Thomas Aquinas, pray for us.

· · · · · · · · · · ·

January 29

[A]s far as the east is from the west,
so far does he remove our transgressions from us.

—PSALM 103:12

Saint Gildas the Wise, pray for us.

· · · · · · · · · · ·

. . . .

January 30

Thanks be to God, especially among young people, many
are rediscovering the value of chastity, which appears
increasingly as a sure guarantee of authentic love.
—POPE BENEDICT XVI

Saint Bathildis, pray for us.

. . . .

January 31

Holy purity, the queen of virtues, the angelic virtue,
is a jewel so precious that those who possess it become
like the angels of God in heaven, even though clothed
in mortal flesh. —SAINT JOHN BOSCO

Saint John Bosco, pray for us.

. . . .

FEBRUARY

- - - - - - - - - - - - - - -

February 1

The fountain of God's love
dwells in pure hearts. —SAINT FAUSTINA KOWALSKA

Saint Brigid of Ireland, pray for us.

- - - - - - - - - - - - - - -

February 2

If you sincerely want to know if you're "going too far,"
don't ask yourself, "Is this bad?" Instead ask yourself,
"Is this pure?" —JASON EVERT

Saint Jeanne de Lestonnac, pray for us.

- - - - - - - - - - - - - - -

February 3

[E]ach man must look within himself to see whether she who
was entrusted to him as a sister in humanity…has not become in
his heart an object of adultery. —POPE JOHN PAUL II

Saint Blase, pray for us.

- - - - - - - - - - - - - - -

. . . .

February 4

Modesty is an unspoken invitation for the guys to be men enough to win our hearts. —CRYSTALINA EVERT

Saint John de Britto, pray for us.

. . . .

February 5

From today onwards, I am going to strive for the greatest purity of soul, that the rays of God's grace may be reflected in all their brilliance. I long to be a crystal in order to find favor in His eyes. —SAINT FAUSTINA KOWALSKA

Saint Agatha, pray for us.

. . . .

February 6

Winning this battle takes faith in Christ, dedication, commitment, honesty with ourselves and others, and a willingness to make sacrifices and deny our own selfish desires. But love is not afraid of those things; love *is* those things. —CHRISTOPHER WEST

Saint Paul Miki and Companions, pray for us.

. . . .

. . . .

February 7

Beauty on the outside never gets into the soul, but beauty of the soul reflects itself on the face.

—ARCHBISHOP FULTON SHEEN

Saint Richard of Lucca, pray for us.

. . . .

February 8

Holy purity is granted by God when it is asked for with humility. —SAINT JOSEMARÍA ESCRIVÁ

Saint Jerome Emiliani, pray for us.

. . . .

February 9

For I know well the plans I have in mind for you, says the LORD, plans for your welfare, not for woe! plans to give you a future full of hope. When you call me, when you go to pray to me, I will listen to you. When you look for me, you will find me. Yes, when you seek me with all your heart, you will find me with you, says the LORD, and I will change your lot. —JEREMIAH 29:11–14, *NAB*

Blessed Marianus Scotus, pray for us.

. . . .

. . . .

February 10

Dress with as much respect as you wish to receive.

—College student

Saint Scholastica, pray for us.

. . . .

February 11

Living purity heals the past. —Jason Evert

Our Lady of Lourdes, pray for us.

. . . .

February 12

To love at all is to be vulnerable. Love anything, and your heart
will certainly be wrung and possibly be broken. If you want to
make sure of keeping it intact, you must give your heart to no
one, not even to an animal. Wrap it carefully round with
hobbies and little luxuries; avoid all entanglements; lock it up
safe in the casket or coffin of your selfishness. But in that
casket—safe, dark, motionless, airless—it will change. It will not
be broken; it will become unbreakable, impenetrable,
irredeemable. —C.S. Lewis

Saint Saturninus and Companions, pray for us.

. . . .

. . . .

February 13

Deep within yourself, listen to your conscience which calls you to be pure. . . . A home is not warmed by the fire of pleasure which burns quickly like a pile of withered grass. Passing encounters are only a caricature of love; they injure hearts and mock God's plan. —POPE JOHN PAUL II

Saint Catherine de Ricci, pray for us.

. . . .

February 14

God wants you to be united to him before you are to be united to another. This is not simply because God deserves your love above anyone else, but because he wants you to be able to express his love. Only then will you be able to truly love anyone in this life. —JASON EVERT

Saint Valentine, pray for us.

. . . .

· · · · · · · · · · · · ·

February 15

Inviting God to write the chapters of our love story involves work on our part—not just a scattered prayer here and there, not merely a feeble attempt to find some insight by flopping open the Bible every now and then. It's seeking Him on a daily basis, putting Him in first place at all times, discovering His heart. —LESLIE LUDY

Saint Claude de la Colombière, pray for us.

· · · · · · · · · · · · ·

February 16

Who shall ascend the hill of the LORD?
And who shall stand in his holy place?
He who has clean hands and a pure heart,
who does not lift up his soul to what is false...

—PSALM 24:3–4

Saint Onesimus, pray for us.

· · · · · · · · · · · · ·

. . . .

February 17
[A man] will be as much of a gentleman as she requires.
—Elizabeth Elliot

Saint Luke Belludi, pray for us.

. . . .

February 18
Temptation is necessary to make us realize that we are
nothing in ourselves. —Saint John Vianney

Saint Simeon, pray for us.

. . . .

February 19
Virginity is the most beautiful thing a man can give his
bride. It sums up the essence of being a man in one choice.
He has promised his whole self, including his body.
—High school female

Saint Conrad of Piacenza, pray for us.

. . . .

. . . .

February 20

[H]old back nothing of yourselves for yourselves so that He
who gives Himself totally to you may receive you totally.

—SAINT FRANCIS OF ASSISI

Saint Eucherius, pray for us.

. . . .

February 21

[T]he most dangerous thing you can do is to take any one
impulse of our own nature and set it up as the thing you
ought to follow at all costs. —C.S. LEWIS

Saint Peter Damian, pray for us.

. . . .

February 22

Many great things depend—don't forget it—on whether
you and I live our lives as God wants.

—SAINT JOSEMARÍA ESCRIVÁ

Saint Peter the Apostle, pray for us.

. . . .

. . . .

February 23

It is not weakness to desire love. The weakness is when we settle for less than love. —CRYSTALINA EVERT

Saint Polycarp, pray for us.

. . . .

February 24

Purity is the fruit of prayer.
—BLESSED TERESA OF CALCUTTA

Saint Ethelbert, pray for us.

. . . .

February 25

Being able to have sex isn't what makes a boy into a man. Anyone can have sex. It's the ability to have self-control that sets the men apart from the boys.
—FEMALE COLLEGE STUDENT

Saint Tarasius, pray for us.

. . . .

. . . .

February 26

We must never forget that only when love between human
beings is put to the test can its true value be seen.

—POPE JOHN PAUL II

Saint Porphyrius, pray for us.

. . . .

February 27

Let no one despise your youth, but set the believers an
example in speech and conduct, in love, in faith, in purity.

—1 TIMOTHY 4:12

Saint Leander, pray for us.

. . . .

February 28

All I ask [of God] is one thing: "Teach me to love. If I love, I
know you'll take care of the rest." —SISTER ROSALIND MOSS

Pope Saint Hilary, pray for us.

. . . .

MARCH

. . . .

March 1

As soon as you willfully allow a dialogue with temptation to begin, the soul is robbed of peace, just as consent to impurity destroys grace. —SAINT JOSEMARÍA ESCRIVÁ

Saint Albinus, pray for us.

. . . .

March 2

Keeping to one woman is a small price for so much as seeing one woman. —G.K. CHESTERTON

Blessed Charles the Good, pray for us.

. . . .

March 3

I can't always cater to what I want because I have to remember what I deserve. —HIGH SCHOOL FEMALE

Saint Katharine Drexel, pray for us.

. . . .

. . . .

March 4

Purity prepares the soul for love, and love confirms the soul in purity. —BLESSED CARDINAL JOHN HENRY NEWMAN

Saint Casimir, pray for us.

. . . .

March 5

Each and every one of us, at the end of the journey of life, will come face to face with either one or the other of two faces.... And one of them, either the merciful face of Christ or the miserable face of Satan, will say, "Mine, mine." May we be Christ's! —ARCHBISHOP FULTON SHEEN

Saint John Joseph of the Cross, pray for us.

. . . .

March 6

In this Sacrament [of reconciliation] . . . you are freed from sin and from its ugly companion which is shame. Your burdens are lifted and you experience the joy of new life in Christ.—POPE JOHN PAUL II

Saint Colette, pray for us.

. . . .

. . . .

March 7

What power we have against temptation if we are able to say, "I choose You, Jesus, because I love You."
—FATHER JEAN C.J. D'ELBÉE

Saints Perpetua and Felicity, pray for us.

. . . .

March 8

[God] assigns the dignity of every woman as a task to every man.—POPE JOHN PAUL II

Saint John of God, pray for us.

. . . .

March 9

Mary, I give you my heart. Always keep it yours. Jesus, Mary, always be my friends. I beg you, let me die rather than be so unfortunate as to commit a single sin.
—SAINT DOMINIC SAVIO

Saint Dominic Savio, pray for us.

. . . .

. . . .

March 10

Never be afraid that some guy is going to leave you unless you give him something sexual. Let *him* be afraid that he's going to lose *you* unless he knows how to respect you.

—CRYSTALINA EVERT

Saint Macarius of Jerusalem, pray for us.

. . . .

March 11

I have never talked about impurity.... But I have spoken many times, as I have to do, about chastity, purity, and the joyful affirmation of love. —SAINT JOSEMARÍA ESCRIVÁ

Saint Eulogius, pray for us.

. . . .

March 12

Be the person you want to marry.

—HIGH SCHOOL FEMALE

Saint Theophanes the Chronicler, pray for us.

. . . .

. . . .

March 13

My grace is sufficient for you, for my power is made perfect
in weakness. —2 CORINTHIANS 12:9

Saint Roderic, pray for us.

. . . .

March 14

Who will pity a snake charmer bitten by a serpent,
or any who go near wild beasts?
So no one will pity a man who associates with a sinner
and becomes involved in his sins....
Flee from sin as from a snake;
for if you approach sin, it will bite you.

—SIRACH 12:13–14; 21:2

Saint Matilda, pray for us.

. . . .

. . . .

March 15

[C]hastity is a difficult, long term matter; one must wait patiently for it to bear fruit, for the happiness of loving kindness which it must bring. But at the same time, chastity is the sure way to happiness. —POPE JOHN PAUL II

Saint Louise de Maríllac, pray for us.

. . . .

March 16

The first requisite for success in your battle with temptations is *firmness of will* joined with *calmness of mind.* —FATHER FRANCIS REMLER

Saint Julian of Antioch, pray for us.

. . . .

March 17

I heard somebody say that you can judge your own character by the things you do in private. I'd take it a step farther and say you can judge your own character by things you do with your girlfriend. —HIGH SCHOOL MALE

Saint Patrick, pray for us.

. . . .

. . . .

March 18

Never talk of impure things or events, not even to deplore them. Look, it's a subject that sticks more than tar. Change the conversation, or if that's not possible, continue, but speaking of the need and beauty of holy purity—a virtue of the men who know what their souls are worth.

—SAINT JOSEMARÍA ESCRIVÁ

Saint Cyril of Jerusalem, pray for us.

. . . .

March 19

Until a man *knows* he's a man he will forever be trying to prove that he is one. —JOHN ELDREDGE

Saint Joseph, pray for us.

. . . .

. . . .

March 20

How can a young man keep his way pure?
By guarding it according to your word.
With my whole heart I seek you;
let me not wander from your commandments!
I have laid up your word in my heart,
that I might not sin against you.

—PSALM 119:9–11

Saint Herbert, pray for us.

. . . .

March 21

Charity is the love of God. There is no other way to
control passion. There is no other route to purity. There is
no other route, finally, to joy. —ELISABETH ELLIOT

Saint Nicholas of Flue, pray for us.

. . . .

. . . .

March 22

So-called sexual freedom is really just proclaiming oneself
to be available for free, and therefore without value. To
"choose" such freedom is tantamount to saying that one is
worth nothing. —SARAH HINLICKY

Saint Basil of Ancyra, pray for us.

. . . .

March 23

"Purity?" they ask. And they smile. They are the ones who
go on to marriage with worn-out bodies and disillusioned
souls. —SAINT JOSEMARÍA ESCRIVÁ

Saint Turibius de Mogrovejo, pray for us.

. . . .

March 24

Because God is love, and we are made in his image and
likeness, our relationships should reflect him in the world.
This, perhaps, is the greatest form of evangelization:
to make an invisible God visible to the world through
our love. —JASON EVERT

Saint Catherine of Sweden, pray for us.

. . . .

· · · · · · · · · · · · ·

March 25

Words are truly the images of the soul. —SAINT BASIL THE GREAT

Saint Dismas, pray for us.

· · · · · · · · · · · · ·

March 26

Girls won't think you're "not a man" if you don't have sex. They will probably trust and respect you more. —HIGH SCHOOL FEMALE

Saint Margaret Clitherow, pray for us.

· · · · · · · · · · · · ·

March 27

If we seriously desire to be pure, we need to realize that it's not the absence of sex that makes us pure. It's the daily desire to glorify God with our bodies. —CRYSTALINA EVERT

Saint Rupert, pray for us.

· · · · · · · · · · · · ·

March 28

[B]y lust I mean that affection of the mind which aims at enjoying one's self and one's neighbor . . . without reference to God. —SAINT AUGUSTINE

Saint Guntramnus, pray for us.

· · · · · · · · · · · · ·

. . . .

March 29

All the temptations of hell cannot stain a soul that does not love them. —Saint Francis de Sales

Saints Jonas and Barachisius, pray for us.

. . . .

March 30

Run from places of sin as from the plague.
—Saint John Climacus

Saint John Climacus, pray for us.

. . . .

March 31

That conversation…was as dirty as a sewer!
It is not enough for you to take no part in it. You must show your repugnance for it strongly!
—Saint Josemaría Escrivá

Saint Benjamin, pray for us.

. . . .

APRIL

. . . .

April 1

One clue that you're doing something wrong is when you start spending a lot of time trying to convince yourself that what you're doing is right. —CRYSTALINA EVERT

Saint Hugh of Grenoble, pray for us.

. . . .

April 2

Man cannot live without love. He remains a being that is incomprehensible for himself, his life is senseless, if love is not revealed to him, if he does not encounter love, if he does not experience it and make it his own, if he does not participate intimately in it. This is why Christ the Redeemer "fully reveals man to himself."

—POPE JOHN PAUL II

Pope John Paul II, pray for us.

. . . .

．　．　．　．　．　．　．　．　．　．　．　．

April 3

The best way to ruin pleasure is to make it your goal.

—J. BUDZISZEWSKI

Saint Richard, pray for us.

．　．　．　．　．　．　．　．　．　．　．　．

April 4

At the foot of the cross, we see Mary, the mother of Jesus, and Saint Mary Magdalene. It is a reminder to us as we look at Mary Magdalene that passion can be transformed by the cross into purity; and with Our Lady, purity is transformed by the cross into passion. What a grace for our world. If they turn to Jesus on the cross, they, too, can be transformed into His image and likeness.

—CARMELITE SISTER OF THE MOST SACRED HEART

Saint Isidore of Seville, pray for us.

．　．　．　．　．　．　．　．　．　．　．　．

. . . .

April 5

Keep the thought of God continually before you, and walk
always in his presence. —SAINT PETER OF ALCANTARA

Saint Vincent Ferrer, pray for us.

. . . .

April 6

This is the will of God, your holiness: that you refrain from
immorality, that each of you know how to acquire a wife for himself
in holiness and honor, not in lustful passion as do the Gentiles who
do not know God.... For God did not call us to impurity but to
holiness. Therefore, whoever disregards this, disregards not a human
being but God, who [also] gives his holy Spirit to you.
—1 THESSALONIANS 4:3–5, 7–8, *NAB*

Saint Marcellinus, pray for us.

. . . .

April 7

If you invoke the Blessed Virgin when you are tempted, she
will come at once to your help, and Satan will leave you.
—SAINT JOHN VIANNEY

Saint John Baptist de la Salle, pray for us.

. . . .

. . . .

April 8

No more baggage, no alcohol, no drugs, no excuses, no hasty rationalizations, no lies, just pure love. I think that's what I've been looking for this whole time. I have to stop running away from the person that God wants me to be.

—HIGH SCHOOL FEMALE

Saint Julia Billiart, pray for us.

. . . .

April 9

Confidently open your most intimate aspirations to the Love of Christ who waits for you in the Eucharist. You will receive the answer to all your worries and you will see with joy that the consistency of your life which he asks of you is the door to fulfill the noblest dreams of your youth.

—POPE JOHN PAUL II

Saint Gaucherius, pray for us.

. . . .

. . . .

April 10

His abstinence from sex is one way to prove his ability to be true to me. I would be so honored to find out that the man I want to marry has respected me enough—without even knowing me—not to have sex with anyone else but me. —HIGH SCHOOL FEMALE

Saint Fulbert, pray for us.

. . . .

April 11

Women, be radiant on your wedding day. But make sure your soul matches your dress. —JASON EVERT

Saint Gemma Galgani, pray for us.

. . . .

April 12

Lust indulged became habit, and habit unresisted became necessity. —SAINT AUGUSTINE

Saint Julius, pray for us.

. . . .

· · · · · · · · · · · · ·

April 13
[H]is mercies never come to an end;
they are new every morning. —LAMENTATIONS 3:22–23

Saint Martin, pray for us.

· · · · · · · · · · · · ·

April 14
I remember the challenge from one female teen on my
radio program who demanded to know, "Why can't I have
sex in a casual way with a number of people if it feels good?
My mother couldn't give me any good reason."…
But, I asked, "Can you feel really good if you know that
ultimately nobody cares about you, nor you about them,
much at all? Isn't that a lonely thought—a lonely feeling?"
She quietly said, "Yes." —DR. LAURA SCHLESSINGER

Saints Tiburtius, Valerius and Maximus, pray for us.

· · · · · · · · · · · · ·

. . . .

April 15

There is need for a crusade of manliness and purity to
counteract and nullify the savage work of those
who think man is a beast.
And that crusade is *your* work. —SAINT JOSEMARÍA ESCRIVÁ

Saint Paternus, pray for us.

. . . .

April 16

The union of body and soul is, in some way, particularly
close in a woman's body.... This is why, when she gives
herself, she gives herself completely; when she stains
herself, the stain is particularly damaging. But Catholicism,
rich in mercy and hope, teaches us that God can make all
things new. —DR. ALICE VON HILDEBRAND

Saint Bernadette of Lourdes, pray for us.

. . . .

April 17

The closer you get to God, the more you become yourself.
—JASON EVERT

Saint Stephen Harding, pray for us.

. . . .

. . . .

April 18

All girls want is a gentleman they can trust.

—High school female

Saint Apollonius, pray for us.

. . . .

April 19

It is better to be single and wish you were married than to be married and wish you were single.

—Father T.G. Morrow

Saint Elphege, pray for us.

. . . .

April 20

[I]mmorality and all impurity... must not even be named among you, as is fitting among saints. —Ephesians 5:3

Saint Marcellinus, pray for us.

. . . .

. . . .

April 21
Purity is reverence paid to the mystery of sex....
[P]urity is the guardian of love.
—Archbishop Fulton Sheen

Saint Anselm, pray for us.

. . . .

April 22
Only when both people see purity as the goal can they be
free to build a relationship based on true love with God as
the center. —Crystalina Evert

Saints Epipodius and Alexander, pray for us.

. . . .

April 23
In order to see Jesus, we first need to let him look at us!
—Pope John Paul II

Saint George, pray for us.

. . . .

. . . .

April 24

I have a lot of regrets right now, but at least I'm not making any more for later. —High school female

Saint Fidelis, pray for us.

. . . .

April 25

Our relentless enemy, the teacher of fornication, whispers that God is lenient and particularly merciful to this passion, since it is so very natural. Yet if we watch the wiles of the demons, we will observe that after we have actually sinned, they will affirm that God is a just and inexorable Judge. They say one thing to lead us into sin, another thing to overwhelm us in despair. —Saint John Climacus

Saint Mark, pray for us.

. . . .

April 26

[S]he who is self-indulgent is dead even while she lives.
—1 Timothy 5:6

Saint Alda, pray for us.

. . . .

. . . .

April 27

When a raven finds a dead body, its first act is to pluck out the eyes; and the first injury that [impurity] inflicts on the soul is to take away the light of the things of God.

—SAINT ALPHONSUS LIGUORI

Saint Zita of Lucca, pray for us.

. . . .

April 28

Now is the time to begin to prepare yourself for family life. You cannot fulfill this path if you do not know how to love. To love means to want to perfect yourself and your beloved, to overcome your selfishness, and give yourself completely.

—SAINT GIANNA BERETTA MOLLA

Saint Louis de Montfort and Saint Gianna Beretta Molla, pray for us.

. . . .

. . . .

April 29

If you are what you should be, you will set the whole
world ablaze. —SAINT CATHERINE OF SIENA

Saint Catherine of Siena, pray for us.

. . . .

April 30

It is not always in the soul's power not to feel a temptation.
But it is always in its power not to consent to it.
—SAINT FRANCIS DE SALES

Saint Pius V, pray for us.

. . . .

MAY

. . . .

May 1

It is the boast of the Catholic Religion that it has the gift of making
the young heart chaste; and why is this, but that it gives us Jesus
Christ for our food, and Mary for our nursing Mother?
—BLESSED CARDINAL JOHN HENRY NEWMAN

Saint Joseph the Worker, pray for us.

. . . .

May 2

The greater the feeling of responsibility for the person
the more true love there is. —POPE JOHN PAUL II

Saint Athanasius, pray for us.

. . . .

May 3

Love waits to give, but lust can't wait to get.
—DRS. HENRY CLOUD AND JOHN TOWNSEND

Saints Timothy and Maura, pray for us.

. . . .

. . . .

May 4

A lot of girls like myself find it geeky when a guy is scared
if they're a virgin. They should be proud.

—HIGH SCHOOL FEMALE

Carthusian Martyrs, pray for us.

. . . .

May 5

Instead of looking for the ideal man, become the ideal
woman and let him come find you.

—CRYSTALINA EVERT

Saint Judith, pray for us.

. . . .

May 6

Before, by yourself, you couldn't. Now, you've turned to our
Lady, and with her, how easy! —SAINT JOSEMARÍA ESCRIVÁ

Blessed Edward Jones, pray for us.

. . . .

. . . .

May 7

I do not fear devils, for thou [Mary] art more powerful
than the whole of Hell. —SAINT ALPHONSUS LIGUORI

Saint John of Beverley, pray for us.

. . . .

May 8

Like a golden ring in a swine's snout
is a beautiful woman with a rebellious disposition....
Charm is deceptive and beauty fleeting;
the woman who fears the LORD is to be praised.

—PROVERBS 11:22; 31:30, *NAB*

Saint Peter of Tarantaise, pray for us.

. . . .

May 9

Have confidence. Return. Invoke our Lady and you'll
be faithful. —SAINT JOSEMARÍA ESCRIVÁ

Saint Pachomius, pray for us.

. . . .

. . . .

May 10

Cling to Mary if you wish to be pure, for she will always
keep you close to God, and with him all things are possible.
—JASON EVERT

Saint Solange, pray for us.

. . . .

May 11

The spotless purity of John's whole life makes him strong
facing the cross. The rest of the Apostles flee from
Golgotha. He, with the Mother of Christ, remains.
Don't forget that purity strengthens and invigorates your
character. —SAINT JOSEMARÍA ESCRIVÁ

Saint Ignatius of Laconi, pray for us.

. . . .

May 12

[B]y not having sex before marriage, you are insisting on your right
to take these things seriously, when many around you do not seem
to. By reserving a part of you for someone else, you are insisting on
your right to keep something sacred. —WENDY SHALIT

Saint Pancras, pray for us.

. . . .

. . . .

May 13

More souls go to hell because of sins of the flesh than for any reason. —OUR LADY OF FATIMA

Our Lady of Fatima, pray for us.

. . . .

May 14

[Pornography] brings intense disappointment, precisely because it is not what I'm really searching for. It's rather like a hungry person standing outside the window of a restaurant, thinking that they're going to get fed. —SINGLE MALE

Saint Matthias, pray for us.

. . . .

May 15

When we were little, we kept close to our mother in a dark alley or if dogs barked at us.
Now, when we feel temptations of the flesh, we should run to the side of our Mother in Heaven, by realizing how close she is to us, and by means of aspirations.
She will defend us and lead us to the light.
—SAINT JOSEMARÍA ESCRIVÁ

Saint Dymphna, pray for us.

. . . .

. . . .

May 16

[A]part from me you can do nothing. —JOHN 15:5

Saint Simon Stock, pray for us.

. . . .

May 17

If you have to lower your morals to find love, then it is not love that you are finding. —JASON EVERT

Saint Pascal Baylon, pray for us.

. . . .

May 18

Be courageous, fear nothing, and you will not be disappointed. —POPE JOHN PAUL II

Pope Saint John I, pray for us.

. . . .

. . . .

May 19

Love our Lady. And she will obtain abundant grace to help
you conquer in your daily struggle. And the enemy will gain
nothing by those perversities that seem to boil up
continually within you.... —SAINT JOSEMARÍA ESCRIVÁ

Pope Saint Celestine, pray for us.

. . . .

May 20

If you see a girl dressed modestly, tell her you appreciate
her modesty. —HIGH SCHOOL FEMALE

Saint Bernardine of Siena, pray for us.

. . . .

May 21

[T]o the penitent he provides a way back,
he encourages those who are losing hope!

. . .

Turn again to the Most High and away from sin.
—SIRACH 17:19, 21, *NAB*

Saint Godric of Finchale, pray for us.

. . . .

. . . .

May 22

Purity shows integrity. You're not arousing the person and then slamming on the brakes. Instead, you're inviting them to love. If they run from the challenge, then you're better off without them. —CRYSTALINA EVERT

Saint Rita of Cascia, pray for us.

. . . .

May 23

We will not be fulfilled in a relationship until we allow the love of Christ to fulfill our desires. —HIGH SCHOOL FEMALE

Saint John Baptist de Rossi, pray for us.

. . . .

May 24

Young love is a flame; very pretty, very hot and fierce, but still only light and flickering. The love of the older and disciplined heart is as coals, deep-burning, unquenchable. —HENRY WARD BEECHER

Saint Donatian, pray for us.

. . . .

. . . .

May 25

Love can only reach maturity when it surpasses how the other person makes me *feel* to arrive at who the other person *is*. —CHRISTOPHER WEST

Saint Mary Magdalene de Pazzi, pray for us.

. . . .

May 26

Humility is the safeguard of chastity. In the matter of purity, there is no greater danger than one not fearing danger of falling. It is almost an infallible sign that he will fall, and with great danger to his soul. —SAINT PHILIP NERI

Saint Philip Neri, pray for us.

. . . .

May 27

Four instincts deeply imbedded in the human heart [are]: affection for the beautiful; admiration for purity; reverence for a Queen; and love of a Mother. All of these come to a focus in Mary. —ARCHBISHOP FULTON SHEEN

Saint Augustine of Canterbury, pray for us.

. . . .

. . . .

May 28

May I give you some advice for you to put into practice
daily? When your heart makes you feel those low cravings,
say slowly to the Immaculate Virgin: Look on me with
compassion. Don't abandon me, my Mother!
—And recommend this prayer to others.
—SAINT JOSEMARÍA ESCRIVÁ

Saint Germanus, pray for us.

. . . .

May 29

[T]ake every thought captive to obey Christ…
—2 CORINTHIANS 10:5

Saint Cyril of Caesarea, pray for us.

. . . .

· · · · · · · · · · · · ·

May 30

Mary, Mother of Jesus, give me your heart so beautiful, so
pure, so immaculate, so full of love and humility that I may
be able to receive Jesus in the Bread of Life, love Him as
You loved Him and serve Him as You served Him in the
distressing disguise of the poorest of the poor.
—BLESSED TERESA OF CALCUTTA

Saint Joan of Arc, pray for us.

· · · · · · · · · · · · ·

May 31

Especially with true devotion to the Blessed Virgin Mary,
anyone can obtain the purity that is a requirement
of real love. —JASON EVERT

Mary, Mediatrix of all graces, pray for us.

· · · · · · · · · · · · ·

JUNE

. . . .

June 1

Real love is demanding. I would fail in my mission if I did not clearly tell you so. Love demands effort and a personal commitment to the will of God. —POPE JOHN PAUL II

Saint Justin Martyr, pray for us.

. . . .

June 2

Bad company ruins good morals. —1 CORINTHIANS 15:33

Saints Peter and Marcellinus, pray for us.

. . . .

June 3

[T]he one obstacle that can turn our lives to misery is the refusal to believe that God will give us the victory of perfect chastity. —FATHER PAUL QUAY

Saint Charles Lwanga, pray for us.

. . . .

. . . .

June 4

If I wasn't respecting my own body, how was he supposed
to respect it? —CRYSTALINA EVERT

Saint Francis Caracciolo, pray for us.

. . . .

June 5

For everyone, whatever his state—single, married, widowed
or priest—chastity is a triumphant affirmation of love.
—SAINT JOSEMARÍA ESCRIVÁ

Saint Boniface, pray for us.

. . . .

June 6

When a man and a woman are united by true love, each
one takes on the destiny, the future of the other, as his or
her own. —POPE JOHN PAUL II

Saint Norbert, pray for us.

. . . .

. . . .

June 7

Love is patient and kind; love is not jealous or boastful; it is not arrogant or rude. Love does not insist on its own way; it is not irritable or resentful; it does not rejoice at wrong, but rejoices in the right. Love bears all things, believes all things, hopes all things, endures all things....

Love never ends...

—1 CORINTHIANS 13:4–8

Saint Willibald, pray for us.

. . . .

June 8

[P]urity doesn't annihilate erotic desire, it perfects it.

—CHRISTOPHER WEST

Saint Medard, pray for us.

. . . .

June 9

Intense love does not measure...it just gives.

—BLESSED TERESA OF CALCUTTA

Saint Ephrem of Syria, pray for us.

. . . .

. . . .

June 10

Don't worry about finding your soul mate in high school.
Find yourself. —Jason Evert

Saint Getulius and Companions, pray for us.

. . . .

June 11

The fashions of the day are all geared toward destroying
women's sensitivity for the dignity of their sex.
—Dr. Alice von Hildebrand

Saint Barnabas, pray for us.

. . . .

June 12

Do not…stir up love before its own time.
—Song of Songs 2:7; 3:5; 8:4 NAB

Pope Saint Leo III, pray for us.

. . . .

. . . .

June 13

Instead of asking God to take the desires away from me altogether, I need to focus more on praying that he will help me to deal with them in a way that is good and pleasing to him. —HIGH SCHOOL FEMALE

Saint Anthony of Padua, pray for us.

. . . .

June 14

As the pilot of a vessel is tried in the storm; as the wrestler is tried in the ring; the soldier in battle, and the hero in adversity: so is the Christian tried in temptation.
—SAINT BASIL THE GREAT

Saint Methodius, pray for us.

. . . .

June 15

The patient girl gets the prize. —JASON EVERT

Saint Germaine Cousin, pray for us.

. . . .

. . . .

June 16

Pure and perfect love does not mean that we are to be free
from temptations, but that we resolutely set our face
against them and refuse to offend God by yielding to them.
—FATHER FRANCIS REMLER

Saint John Francis Regis, pray for us.

. . . .

June 17

If you want a man to respect you, and perhaps eventually
fall in love with you, then you must show him that you
respect yourself and that you recognize your dignity
before God. —MIKE MATHEWS

Saint Albert Chmielowski, pray for us.

. . . .

June 18

If a man loves a woman, he will wait for her. Not only that,
he will wait *with* her. He should focus on guarding her
purity as well as his own. —CRYSTALINA EVERT

Saint Elizabeth of Schönau, pray for us.

. . . .

. . . .

June 19

When impure thoughts come into our minds, we should
think of them as little as we do of the leaves that fall from
the trees. We must not dwell on them for a moment and,
without heeding such suggestions from the enemy of souls,
go quietly on our way. —SAINT CLEMENT HOFBAUER

Saint Romuald, pray for us.

. . . .

June 20

[Young people] know that their life *has meaning to the extent
that it becomes a free gift for others.* —POPE JOHN PAUL II

Saint Silverius, pray for us.

. . . .

June 21

If a relationship is holding you back spiritually, this is an
unmistakable sign that the relationship is not of God.
—JASON EVERT

Saint Aloysius Gonzaga, pray for us.

. . . .

. . . .

June 22

Don't say, "That's the way I am—it's my character."
It's your *lack* of character. *Esto vir!*—Be a man!
—SAINT JOSEMARÍA ESCRIVÁ

Saint Thomas More, pray for us.

. . . .

June 23

Girls may be confusing to guys, but mostly it's simple:
We want to be loved. —HIGH SCHOOL FEMALE

Saint Audrey, pray for us.

. . . .

June 24

Occupy your minds with good thoughts, or the enemy will
fill them with bad ones. —SAINT THOMAS MORE

Saint John the Baptist, pray for us.

. . . .

. . . .

June 25

Jesus has made Himself the Bread of Life to give us life.
Night and day, He is there. If you really want to grow in
love, come back to the Eucharist, come back to that
Adoration. —BLESSED TERESA OF CALCUTTA

Saint Prosper of Aquitaine, pray for us.

. . . .

June 26

Many live like angels in the middle of the world. You,...
why not you? —SAINT JOSEMARÍA ESCRIVÁ

Saint Josemaría Escrivá, pray for us.

. . . .

June 27

If you have to ask someone if he'll still love you tomorrow,
then he doesn't love you tonight. —DAWN EDEN

Saint Cyril of Alexandria, pray for us.

. . . .

. . . .

June 28

[W]hen you come to serve the LORD,
prepare yourself for trials.
Be sincere of heart and steadfast,
undisturbed in time of adversity.
Cling to him, forsake him not;
thus will your future be great.
Accept whatever befalls you,
in crushing misfortune be patient;
For in fire gold is tested,
and worthy men in the crucible of humiliation.
Trust God and he will help you;
make straight your ways and hope in him.

You who fear the LORD, wait for his mercy,
turn not away lest you fall.

—SIRACH 2:1–7, *NAB*

Saint Irenaeus, pray for us.

. . . .

. . . .

June 29

Always remain close to the Catholic Church, because it
alone can give you true peace, since it alone possesses Jesus
in the Blessed Sacrament, the true Prince of Peace.

—Saint Padre Pio

Saints Peter and Paul, pray for us.

. . . .

June 30

[W]hen marriage exposes a person's selfishness and sins it's
doing what it is *meant* to do: bringing our sins and wounds
to light so we can recognize them, confess them, and begin
the healing process. —Christopher West

First Martyrs of Rome, pray for us.

. . . .

JULY

· · · · · · · · · · · ·

July 1

Don't say that you have a chaste mind if you have unchaste eyes, because an unchaste eye is the messenger of an unchaste heart. —SAINT AUGUSTINE

Blessed Junípero Serra, pray for us.

· · · · · · · · · · · ·

July 2

When a relationship begins the right way—with a long, God-centered friendship—there probably won't be any need to tell the guy no: He will be enough of a man of God to lead you to purity. Finding a man like this is not a ridiculous dream. It's a standard. —CRYSTALINA EVERT

Saint Bernardino Realino, pray for us.

· · · · · · · · · · · ·

July 3

Behold, I make all things new. —REVELATION 21:5

Saint Thomas the Apostle, pray for us.

· · · · · · · · · · · ·

. . . .

July 4

With all the strength of my soul I urge you young people to approach the Communion table as often as you can. Feed on this bread of angels whence you will draw all the energy you need to fight inner battles. Because true happiness, dear friends, does not consist in the pleasures of the world or in earthly things, but in peace of conscience, which we only have if we are pure in heart and mind.

—Blessed Pier Giorgio Frassati

Blessed Pier Giorgio Frassati, pray for us.

. . . .

July 5

Purity is not about following a list of rules so that you'll avoid hell. It's about wanting heaven for the person you love. —Jason Evert

Saint Anthony Zaccaria, pray for us.

. . . .

. . . .

July 6

If I looked at porn, I wouldn't be able to honestly say to myself that the reason I am attracted to any woman is the reason that God wants. Or I might not even be able to tell if it really was love. It's like it would cheapen everything that I like in the few pure-hearted girls that I know.
—HIGH SCHOOL MALE

Saint María Goretti, pray for us.

. . . .

July 7

If you say the Holy Rosary every day, with a spirit of faith and love, our Lady will make sure she leads you very far along her Son's path. —SAINT JOSEMARÍA ESCRIVÁ

Blessed Ralph Milner, pray for us.

. . . .

July 8

One of the greatest forms of affection is friendship.
—BLESSED PIER GIORGIO FRASSATI

Saint Grimbald, pray for us.

. . . .

. . . .

July 9

After I got over him, which took a pretty long time, I
realized what I was looking so hard for before I met him:
myself. —FEMALE COLLEGE STUDENT

Saint Veronica Giuliani, pray for us.

. . . .

July 10

There is no place for selfishness—and no place for fear! Do
not be afraid, then, when love makes demands. Do not be
afraid when love requires sacrifice. —POPE JOHN PAUL II

Saints Rufina and Secunda, pray for us.

. . . .

July 11

A temptation that is resisted, far from doing harm to your
soul, becomes the means of *great spiritual gain*. It directly
promotes growth in virtue, in the love of God, in grace, and
in merit for Heaven. —FATHER FRANCIS REMLER

Saint Benedict, pray for us.

. . . .

. . . .

July 12

The only place outside Heaven where you can be perfectly safe from all the dangers and perturbations of love is Hell.
—C.S. LEWIS

Saint John Gualbert, pray for us.

. . . .

July 13

[I thought] about what I should be doing as the male in the relationship. I should be preparing her and helping her become a handmaiden of the Lord, rather than taking her away from him. —HIGH SCHOOL MALE

Saint Henry II, pray for us.

. . . .

July 14

[T]hough your sins are like scarlet,
   they shall be as white as snow;
   though they are red like crimson,
they shall become like wool. —ISAIAH 1:18

Saint Camillus de Lellis, pray for us.

. . . .

. . . .

July 15

Men do not fear a great army, as the powers of hell fear the name and protection of Mary. —Saint Bonaventure

Saint Bonaventure, pray for us.

. . . .

July 16

[C]haste woman plus unchaste clothing equals instant hypocrite. —Dawn Eden

Our Lady of Mount Carmel, pray for us.

. . . .

July 17

Let the enemy rage at the gate; let him knock, pound, scream, howl; let him do his worst. We know for certain that he cannot enter our soul except by the door of our consent. —Saint Francis de Sales

Blessed Martyrs of Compiegne, pray for us.

. . . .

. . . .

July 18

Be sober, be watchful. Your adversary the devil prowls around like a roaring lion, seeking some one to devour. Resist him, firm in your faith, knowing that the same experience of suffering is required of your brotherhood throughout the world. And after you have suffered a little while, the God of all grace, who has called you to his eternal glory in Christ, will himself restore, establish, and strengthen you. —1 PETER 5:8–10

Saint Frederick, pray for us.

. . . .

July 19

By valuing her own purity, the girl can help the guy understand that her body is a treasure to be cherished, not some goal to be conquered. —CRYSTALINA EVERT

Saint Arsenius, pray for us.

. . . .

. . . .

July 20

The devil is like a rabid dog tied to a chain; beyond the length of the chain he cannot seize anyone. And you: keep at a distance. If you approach too near, you let yourself be caught. Remember that the devil has only one door by which to enter the soul: the will. —SAINT PADRE PIO

Saint Margaret of Antioch, pray for us.

. . . .

July 21

The person who does not decide to love forever will find it very difficult to really love for even one day.
—POPE JOHN PAUL II

Saint Lawrence of Brindisi, pray for us.

. . . .

July 22

[W]omen imbued with a spirit of the Gospel can do so much to aid humanity in not falling. —VATICAN II

Saint Mary Magdalene, pray for us.

. . . .

. . . .

July 23

When you see the storm coming, if you seek safety in that firm refuge which is Mary, there will be no danger of your wavering or going down. —SAINT JOSEMARÍA ESCRIVÁ

Saint Bridget of Sweden, pray for us.

. . . .

July 24

Sacrifices made out of love for one another bring a couple closer than any pleasure on earth. —JASON EVERT

Saint John Boste, pray for us.

. . . .

July 25

[A young heart feels] a desire for greater generosity, more commitment, greater love. This desire for more is characteristic of youth; a heart that is in love does not calculate, does not begrudge, it wants to give of itself without measure. —POPE JOHN PAUL II

Saint Christopher, pray for us.

. . . .

. . . .

July 26
Never commit to a person hoping that he or she will
change. Commit to a person only if you like them exactly as
they are. Otherwise you're committing to an imaginary
person. —Crystalina Evert

Saints Joachim and Anne, pray for us.

. . . .

July 27
Admire not how sinners live,
but trust in the Lord and wait for his light.
—Sirach 11:21, NAB

Pope Saint Celestine I, pray for us.

. . . .

July 28
The lustful gratification never outweighs the morning
sorrow.—High school male

Saint Samson of York, pray for us.

. . . .

. . . .

July 29

Above all, create silence in your interior. Let that ardent
desire to see God arise from the depth of your hearts, a
desire that at times is suffocated by the noise of the world
and the seduction of pleasures. —POPE JOHN PAUL II

Saint Martha, pray for us.

. . . .

July 30

[W]omen who dress immodestly often complain that men
are all "animals." That's because the wild ones come
running while the decent men stay away.
—FATHER T.G. MORROW

Saint Peter Chrysologus, pray for us.

. . . .

. . . .

July 31

Just as the commander of an army pitches his camp, studies
the strength and defenses of a fortress, and then attacks it
on its weakest side, in like manner, the enemy of our
human nature studies from all sides our theological,
cardinal, and moral virtues. Wherever he finds us weakest
and most in need regarding our eternal salvation, he attacks
and tries to take us by storm. —SAINT IGNATIUS OF LOYOLA

Saint Ignatius of Loyola, pray for us.

. . . .

AUGUST

. . . .

August 1

Were you to ask what are the means of overcoming temptations, I would answer: The first means is prayer; the second is prayer; the third is prayer; and should you ask me a thousand times, I would repeat the same.

—SAINT ALPHONSUS LIGUORI

Saint Alphonsus Liguori, pray for us.

. . . .

August 2

Purity is love.

—CRYSTALINA EVERT

Pope Saint Stephen I, pray for us.

. . . .

. . . .

August 3

If little girls were made aware of the great mystery confided to them, their purity would be guaranteed. The very reverence which they would have toward their own bodies would inevitably be perceived by the other sex. Men are talented at reading women's body language, and they are not likely to risk being humiliated when a refusal is certain. Perceiving women's modesty, they would take their cue and, in return, approach the female sex with reverence, instead of with today's brutal irreverence which unleashes lust and impurity. —DR. ALICE VON HILDEBRAND

Saint Lydia, pray for us.

. . . .

August 4

Here is a rule for everyday life: *Do not do anything which you cannot offer to God.* —SAINT JOHN VIANNEY

Saint John Vianney, pray for us.

. . . .

. . . .

August 5

Temptation is a test of love. By fighting well, we prove our loyalties and give glory to God. After a temptation, you will be either closer to God or further from him. The choice lies with you. If you choose well, your reward will be nothing less than God himself. —Jason Evert

Saint Afra, pray for us.

. . . .

August 6

At the time of your examination [of conscience] beware of the devil that ties your tongue. —Saint Josemaría Escrivá

Saint Justus, pray for us.

. . . .

. . . .

August 7

Blessed is the man who endures trial, for when he has stood the test
he will receive the crown of life which God has promised to those
who love him. Let no one say when he is tempted, "I am tempted by
God"; for God cannot be tempted with evil and he himself tempts
no one; but each person is tempted when he is lured and enticed by
his own desire. Then desire when it has conceived gives birth to sin;
and sin when it is full-grown brings forth death. —JAMES 1:12–15

Pope Saint Sixtus II, pray for us.

. . . .

August 8

The standard is not "What's wrong?" The standard is
"Does this lead me closer to God?"—SISTER ROSALIND MOSS

Saint Dominic, pray for us.

. . . .

August 9

Every woman who wants to fulfill her destiny must look to
Mary as the ideal. —SAINT TERESA BENEDICTA OF THE CROSS
(EDITH STEIN)

Saint Teresa Benedicta, pray for us.

. . . .

. . . .

August 10

Always be doing something worthwhile; then the Devil will always find you busy. —Saint Francis of Assisi

Saint Lawrence, pray for us.

. . . .

August 11

It's my job, as a woman, to inspire men to be noble, brave, honorable, and to protect and defend the loveliness and beauty of every woman. —Camille De Blasi

Saint Philomena, pray for us.

. . . .

August 12

Chastity is a virtue which we have not strength to practice unless God gives it to us; and God does not give strength except to him who asks for it. But whoever prays for it will certainly obtain it. —Saint Alphonsus Liguori

Saint Euplius, pray for us.

. . . .

. . . .

August 13

The only guy worth your tears is the one who would never make you cry. —HIGH SCHOOL FEMALE

Saint John Berchmans, pray for us.

. . . .

August 14

The Immaculata [Mary] alone has from God the promise of victory over Satan.... She seeks souls who will consecrate themselves entirely to her, who will become in her hands effective instruments for the defeat of Satan and the spreading of God's kingdom upon earth.

—SAINT MAXIMILIAN MARY KOLBE

Saint Maximilian Mary Kolbe, pray for us.

. . . .

. . . .

August 15

[Mary] is the one whom every man loves when he loves a woman—whether he knows it or not. She is what every woman wants to be when she looks at herself. She is the woman whom every man marries in ideal when he takes a spouse;...she is the secret desire every woman has to be honored and fostered; she is the way every woman wants to command respect and love because of the beauty of her goodness of body and soul. —ARCHBISHOP FULTON SHEEN

Mary, assumed into heaven, pray for us.

. . . .

August 16

The eucharist is a fire which inflames us, that, like lions breathing fire, we may retire from the altar, being made terrible to the devil. —SAINT JOHN CHRYSOSTOM

Saint Stephen the Great, pray for us.

. . . .

. . . .

August 17
Study the generations long past and understand;
has anyone hoped in the LORD and been disappointed?

...

For equal to his majesty
is the mercy that he shows.
—SIRACH 2:10, 18, *NAB*

Saint Hyacinth, pray for us.

. . . .

August 18
If we want to find love, we need to get to know ourselves
before we get to know anyone else. —CRYSTALINA EVERT

Saint Jane Frances de Chantal, pray for us.

. . . .

August 19
Men must be taught to love, and to love in a noble way;
they must be educated in depth in this truth, that is, in the
fact that a woman is a person and not simply an object.
—POPE JOHN PAUL II

Saint John Eudes, pray for us.

. . . .

. . . .

August 20

To defend his purity, Saint Francis of Assisi rolled in the snow, Saint Benedict threw himself into a thornbush, Saint Bernard plunged into an icy pond....

You...what have *you* done? —SAINT JOSEMARÍA ESCRIVÁ

Saint Bernard of Clairvaux, pray for us.

. . . .

August 21

Ceasing to be "in love" need not mean ceasing to love.
—C.S. LEWIS

Pope Saint Pius X, pray for us.

. . . .

August 22

My desire is for the young people of the entire world to come closer to Mary. She is the bearer of an indelible youthfulness and beauty that never wanes. May young people have increasing confidence in her and may they entrust the life just opening before them to her.
—POPE JOHN PAUL II

Mary, Queen of Heaven, pray for us.

. . . .

. . . .

August 23

[A]re men and women willing to pay the price of renunciation, sacrifice, and discipline required to find and live the love that *does* satisfy? The answer to this question will determine the entire course of a person's life.
—CHRISTOPHER WEST

Saint Rose of Lima, pray for us.

. . . .

August 24

[T]he young man who rings the bell at the brothel is unconsciously looking for God. —BRUCE MARSHALL

Saint Bartholomew, pray for us.

. . . .

August 25

The satisfaction of the passions is one thing, and the joy that man finds in mastering himself more fully is another thing.—POPE JOHN PAUL II

Saint Louis, pray for us.

. . . .

. . . .

August 26
The greatest illusion of lovers is to believe that the intensity of their sexual attraction is the guarantee of the perpetuity of their love. —ARCHBISHOP FULTON SHEEN

Saint Elizabeth Bichier des Ages, pray for us.

. . . .

August 27
How shall I speak of a few careless kisses to a generation nurtured on the assumption that nearly everybody goes to bed with everybody? Of those who flounder in the sea of permissiveness and self-indulgence, are there any who still search the sky for the beacon of purity? If I did not believe there were, I would not bother to write. —ELISABETH ELLIOT

Saint Monica, pray for us.

. . . .

August 28
The way one treats a woman corresponds to the way one lives with God. —PHILIPPE LEFEBVRE

Saint Augustine, pray for us.

. . . .

. . . .

August 29

Shun immorality. Every other sin which a man commits is outside the body; but the immoral man sins against his own body. Do you not know that your body is a temple of the Holy Spirit within you, which you have from God? You are not your own; you were bought with a price. So glorify God in your body. —1 CORINTHIANS 6:18–20

Saint Medericus, pray for us.

. . . .

August 30

It takes a lot for a guy to stay a virgin, and I love boys like that—who don't care what people think!

—HIGH SCHOOL FEMALE

Saint Pammachius, pray for us.

. . . .

. . . .

August 31

[Y]oung people are always searching for the beauty in love.
They want their love to be beautiful. If they give in to
weakness, following [worldly] models of behavior...;
in the depths of their hearts they still desire a beautiful and
pure love. This is as true of boys as it is of girls. Ultimately,
they know that only God can give them this love. As a
result, they are willing to follow Christ, without caring
about the sacrifices this may entail. —POPE JOHN PAUL II

Saint Aristedes, pray for us.

. . . .

SEPTEMBER

. . . .

September 1

A pure soul is synonymous with a heart full of love of God.
—SAINT PADRE PIO

Saint Giles, pray for us.

. . . .

September 2

[Each woman] is for the man the master of her own
mystery. —POPE JOHN PAUL II

Saint Ingrid of Sweden, pray for us.

. . . .

September 3

Authentic sexual attraction is always an attraction to the
beauty of the other *as a person*, not merely as an object of
selfish consumption. This is the enormous value of the
virtue of chastity. —CHRISTOPHER WEST

Saint Gregory the Great, pray for us.

. . . .

. . . .

September 4

Purity is trusting God with your body. —JASON EVERT

Saint Rosalia, pray for us.

. . . .

September 5

Of my free will, dear Jesus, I shall follow You wherever You shall go in search of souls, at any cost to myself and out of pure love of You. —BLESSED TERESA OF CALCUTTA

Blessed Teresa of Calcutta, pray for us.

. . . .

September 6

Once you allow yourself to be defined by your loneliness, it's a small step to violating your most deeply held beliefs. —DAWN EDEN

Blessed Bertrand, pray for us.

. . . .

. . . .

September 7

Take care, then, not consciously to do or say anything which, if all the world were to know it, you could not acknowledge and say, "Yes, that was what I did or that was what I said." —SAINT LOUIS IX OF FRANCE

Saint Regina, pray for us.

. . . .

September 8

A saint has compared those who have kept their hearts pure, to the lilies that, rising heavenwards on their tall stems, fill the air with fragrance. The mere sight of them makes us think of purity. Even so the Blessed Virgin inspired with purity all who looked at her.

—SAINT JOHN VIANNEY

Saint Mary, pray for us.

. . . .

September 9

Your relationships should be a reflection of God's love, not a replacement for it. —CRYSTALINA EVERT

Saint Peter Claver, pray for us.

. . . .

. . . .

September 10

A guy can respect you more if he respects himself.
—HIGH SCHOOL FEMALE

Saint Nicholas of Tolentino, pray for us.

. . . .

September 11

Although I have lived through much darkness,... I have seen enough evidence to be unshakably convinced that no difficulty, no fear is so great that it can completely suffocate the hope that springs eternal in the hearts of the young.... Do not let that hope die! Stake your lives on it! We are not the sum of our weaknesses and failures; we are the sum of the Father's love for us and our real capacity to become the image of his Son.—POPE JOHN PAUL II

Saint Adelphus, pray for us.

. . . .

September 12

When you feel far from God and far from everything that you wanted to be for him, realize that you still have your whole future to give him.—JASON EVERT

Blessed Apollinar Franco, pray for us.

. . . .

. . . .

September 13

[A young husband should say to his bride], I have taken you in my arms, and I love you, and I prefer you to my life itself. For the present life is nothing, and my most ardent dream is to spend it with you in such a way that we may be assured of not being separated in the life reserved for us (CCC, 2365, quoting Homilies in Ephesians, 20, 8).

—SAINT JOHN CHRYSOSTOM

Saint John Chrysostom, pray for us.

. . . .

September 14

The sign of the cross is the most terrible weapon against the Devil. Thus the Church wishes not only that we should have it continually in front of our minds to recall to us just what our souls are worth and what they cost Jesus Christ, but also that we should make it at every juncture ourselves: when we go to bed, when we awaken during the night, when we get up, when we begin any action, and, above all, when we are tempted. —SAINT JOHN VIANNEY

Saints Caerealis and Sallustia, pray for us.

. . . .

.   .   .   .

September 15

Some girls fear, "What if I wait for marriage, and he never comes?" But what if he waits, and you never show up? What if you lower your standards to find him, and the good one passes you by? You'll always wonder what could have been. Be pure, and let God take care of the details.

—JASON EVERT

Saint Catherine of Genoa, pray for us.

.   .   .   .

September 16

Chastity can only be thought of in association with the virtue of love. —POPE JOHN PAUL II

Saint Cornelius, pray for us.

.   .   .   .

September 17

[F]lee idleness... for no one is more exposed to such temptations than he who has nothing to do.

—SAINT ROBERT BELLARMINE

Saint Robert Bellarmine, pray for us.

.   .   .   .

. . . .

September 18

If you remembered the presence of your Angel and the angels of your neighbors, you would avoid many of the foolish things which slip into your conversations.
—SAINT JOSEMARÍA ESCRIVÁ

Saint Joseph of Cupertino, pray for us.

. . . .

September 19

No man is able to love a woman as his bride without first loving her as his sister. —JASON EVERT

Saint Emily de Rodat, pray for us.

. . . .

September 20

[W]hen you put on chastity, you'll discover a life more hope-filled, more vibrant, more real than anything you might have experienced when having sex outside of marriage. *That* is the thrill of the chaste. —DAWN EDEN

Saints Andrew Kim, Paul Chong and Companions, pray for us.

. . . .

. . . .

September 21

Blessed are the pure in heart, for they shall see God.

—MATTHEW 5:8

Saint Matthew, pray for us.

. . . .

September 22

If you constantly worry that a guy will reject you unless you give him something sexual, you're missing the chance to invite him to become a man. It is here, where you think you're the weakest, that you really have the most power.

—CRYSTALINA EVERT

Saint Thomas of Villanova, pray for us.

. . . .

September 23

Don't let temptations frighten you; they are the trials of the souls whom God wants to test when he sees they have the necessary strength to sustain the struggle, thus weaving the crown of glory with their own hands.

—SAINT PADRE PIO

Saint Padre Pío, pray for us.

. . . .

. . . .

September 24
An impure heart is neither satisfied nor free.
—JOHANN CHRISTOPH ARNOLD

Saint Pacifico of San Severino, pray for us.

. . . .

September 25
[L]ove…is victorious because it prays.
—POPE JOHN PAUL II

Saint Finbar, pray for us.

. . . .

September 26
The preservation of innocence is not due to prudery, to
fear, to love of isolation, but to a passionate desire to
preserve a secret until God gives the one to whom it can be
whispered. —ARCHBISHOP FULTON SHEEN

Saints Cosmas and Damian, pray for us.

. . . .

. . . .

September 27

Strive for the purity of angels, and you will find the peace and joy that they have. —JASON EVERT

Saint Vincent de Paul, pray for us.

. . . .

September 28

[O]nly in silence does man succeed in hearing in the depth of his conscience the voice of God, which really makes him free. —POPE JOHN PAUL II

Saint Wenceslaus, pray for us.

. . . .

September 29

I have great reverence for Saint Michael the Archangel; he had no example to follow in doing the will of God, and yet he fulfilled God's will faithfully. —SAINT FAUSTINA KOWALSKA

Saints Michael, Gabriel and Raphael, Archangels, pray for us.

. . . .

. . . .

September 30

[W]e must either speak as we are dressed, or else dress as we speak. Why do we profess one thing and practice another? The tongue talks of chastity, but the rest of the body reveals [impurity]. —SAINT JEROME

Saint Jerome, pray for us.

. . . .

OCTOBER

. . . .

October 1

Sufferings gladly borne for others convert more people
than sermons. —SAINT THÉRÈSE OF LISIEUX

Saint Thérèse of Lisieux, pray for us.

. . . .

October 2

If only we could see the *joy* of our guardian angel when he
sees us fighting our temptations! —SAINT JOHN VIANNEY

Guardian Angels, pray for us.

. . . .

October 3

A woman with the courage to step out into the unknown, risking
temporary loneliness for a shot at lasting joy, is more than a "single."
She's *singular.* Instead of defining herself by what she lacks—
a relationship with a man—she defines herself by what she has:
a relationship with God. —DAWN EDEN

Saint Gerard of Brogne, pray for us.

. . . .

. . . .

October 4

Temptation overcome is in a way a ring with which the Lord espouses the soul of his servant to himself.

—SAINT FRANCIS OF ASSISI

Saint Francis of Assisi, pray for us.

. . . .

October 5

A soul does not benefit as it should from the sacrament of confession if it is not humble. Pride keeps it in darkness. The soul neither knows how, nor is it willing, to probe with precision the depths of its own misery. It puts on a mask and avoids everything that might bring it recovery.

—SAINT FAUSTINA KOWALSKA

Saint Faustina, pray for us.

. . . .

October 6

A man who has the habit of abusive language will never mature in character as long as he lives.

—SIRACH 23:15, *NAB*

Saint Bruno, pray for us.

. . . .

. . . .

October 7

The holy Rosary is a powerful weapon. Use it with
confidence and you'll be amazed at the results.
—SAINT JOSEMARÍA ESCRIVÁ

Our Lady of the Rosary, pray for us.

. . . .

October 8

Ultimately, it seems that only men can teach other men
how to behave around women, but those men have to be
inspired by women in the first place, inspired enough to
think the women are worth being courteous to.
—WENDY SHALIT

Saint Pelagia, pray for us.

. . . .

October 9

A woman should hide her heart in God, and [the man]
must go there to find it. —HIGH SCHOOL FEMALE

Saint Denis, pray for us.

. . . .

. . . .

October 10

[P]urity of heart and body must be defended, because chastity "safeguards" authentic love. —POPE JOHN PAUL II

Saint Francis Borgia, pray for us.

. . . .

October 11

Invite Christ and his angels to witness every moment of your life and every expression of your love. —JASON EVERT

Saint Firminus, pray for us.

. . . .

October 12

Don't be afraid to be a virgin. —HIGH SCHOOL FEMALE

Saint Wilfrid, pray for us.

. . . .

October 13

[C]ertain fashions will be introduced that will offend Our Lord very much. —OUR LADY OF FATIMA, IN 1920

Saint Edward the Confessor, pray for us.

. . . .

. . . .

October 14

Daily Mass is for those who have nothing better to do, which means all of us. —JASON EVERT

Pope Saint Callistus I, pray for us.

. . . .

October 15

Never do anything that you cannot do in the presence of all. —SAINT TERESA OF AVILA

Saint Teresa of Avila, pray for us.

. . . .

October 16

God therefore "touches" the female body in placing this new soul into the temple of her womb.
—DR. ALICE VON HILDEBRAND

Saint Gerard Majella, pray for us.

. . . .

. . . .

October 17

[W]hatever is true, whatever is honorable, whatever is just, whatever is pure…think about these things.

—PHILIPPIANS 4:8

Saint Ignatius of Antioch, pray for us.

. . . .

October 18

The search and discovery of God's will for you is a deep and fascinating endeavor. Every vocation, every path to which Christ calls us, ultimately leads to fulfillment and happiness, because it leads to God, to sharing in God's own life.—POPE JOHN PAUL II

Saint Luke, pray for us.

. . . .

October 19

Purity never ruins loving relationships. If the relationship is based on lust, purity will end it. But if the relationship is based on love, purity will save it. —CRYSTALINA EVERT

Saints Isaac Jogues, John de Brébeuf and Companions, pray for us.

. . . .

. . . .

October 20

The woman who says no to her boyfriend when he asks for immoral activity is showing him love.

—FATHER T.G. MORROW

Saint Paul of the Cross, pray for us.

. . . .

October 21

[S]ay the Holy Rosary. Blessed be that monotony of Hail Marys which purifies the monotony of your sins!

—SAINT JOSEMARÍA ESCRIVÁ

Saint Hilarion, pray for us.

. . . .

October 22

I don't hook up; I have morals, and I'm not ashamed of them. If you don't respect that, then go home.

—HIGH SCHOOL FEMALE

Saint Mary Salome, pray for us.

. . . .

. . . .

October 23

Self-confident people who strive for purity in their own strength will always be stumbling. Humble people, on the other hand, live in God's strength. They may fall, but God will always lift them up. —JOHANN CHRISTOPH ARNOLD

Saint John of Capistrano, pray for us.

. . . .

October 24

The pure man perceives the mystery of sex. He perceives its depth, its seriousness, its intimacy.... [And] it is only by divine permission that he lifts the veil from this mystery.
—DIETRICH VON HILDEBRAND

Saint Anthony Mary Claret, pray for us.

. . . .

October 25

To begin is for everyone, to persevere is for saints.
—SAINT JOSEMARÍA ESCRIVÁ

Saint Gaudentius, pray for us.

. . . .

. . . .

October 26

God help the man who won't marry until he finds a perfect
woman, and God help him still more if he finds her.

—BENJAMIN TILLETT

Saint Evaristus, pray for us.

. . . .

October 27

When considering your faults and virtues, look carefully at
whom you compare yourself to. If you compare yourself
with those far from God, you will become more like them.
Compare yourself to the saints if you want to become one.

—JASON EVERT

Saint Frumentius, pray for us.

. . . .

October 28

Modesty, on the other hand, instead of treating men like
dogs, invites them to consider an idea. —WENDY SHALIT

Saint Jude, pray for us.

. . . .

.   .   .   .

October 29

Let us not grow tired of doing good, for in due time we
shall reap our harvest, if we do not give up.

—GALATIANS 6:9, *NAB*

Saint Narcissus, pray for us.

.   .   .   .

October 30

Persevere. The harder the climb, the greater the view will
be when you get to the top. —JASON EVERT

Saint Alphonsus Rodríguez, pray for us.

.   .   .   .

October 31

You always leave the Rosary for later, and you end up not
saying it at all because you are sleepy. —If there is no other
time, say it in the street without letting anybody notice it.
It will, moreover, help you to have presence of God.

—SAINT JOSEMARÍA ESCRIVÁ

Saint Quentin, pray for us.

.   .   .   .

NOVEMBER

. . . .

November 1

Follow the saints, because those who follow them will become saints. —POPE SAINT CLEMENT I

All you holy saints, pray for us

. . . .

November 2

Where is your security? If it is in him, then your sadness makes sense. But if it is in Him, then your heart will be filled with peace. —HIGH SCHOOL FEMALE

Saint Eustachius, pray for us.

. . . .

November 3

It's ironic that one minute we're saying that no guy would want a pure girl, and the next minute we're saying that no guy would want us because we're not pure.
—CRYSTALINA EVERT

Saint Martin de Porres, pray for us.

. . . .

．．．．．．．．．．．．．．

November 4

Love between man and woman cannot be built without sacrifices and self-denial. —POPE JOHN PAUL II

Saint Charles Borromeo, pray for us.

．．．．．．．．．．．．．．

November 5

[W]oman is the conscience of man. —SØREN KIERKEGAARD

Saint Sylvia, pray for us.

．．．．．．．．．．．．．．

November 6

In failing to confess, Lord, I would only hide You from myself, not myself from You. —SAINT AUGUSTINE

Saint Leonard, pray for us.

．．．．．．．．．．．．．．

. . . .

November 7

Do not conform yourselves to this age but be transformed
by the renewal of your mind, that you may discern what is
the will of God, what is good and pleasing and perfect.

—ROMANS 12:2, *NAB*

Saint Carina and Companions, pray for us.

. . . .

November 8

Love finds nothing hard: no task is difficult if you
wish to do it.—SAINT JEROME

Saint Godfrey, pray for us.

. . . .

November 9

In a man, the mystery [of sexuality] is revealed in chivalry
to women, not because he believes that woman is physically
weaker but because of the awe he feels in the presence
of mystery. —ARCHBISHOP FULTON SHEEN

Saint Alexander, pray for us.

. . . .

. . . .

November 10

Love alone has the power to consistently overcome the temptations of lust. Shame and fear may motivate a person for some time to be abstinent, but they cannot win the war for true and lasting purity. —JASON EVERT

Saint Leo the Great, pray for us.

. . . .

November 11

Temptation is necessary to make us realize that we are nothing in ourselves. —SAINT JOHN VIANNEY

Saint Martin of Tours, pray for us.

. . . .

November 12

Now, Lord, you know that I take this wife of mine
not because of lust,
but for a noble purpose.
Call down your mercy on me and on her,
and allow us to live together to a happy old age.
—TOBIT 8:7, NAB

Saint Josaphat, pray for us.

. . . .

. . . .

November 13

Every resistance to a temptation is equivalent to an act of divine love. And the more violent our temptations are, and the longer they last, the more ample opportunities do they furnish us for exhibiting our love of God in the very highest degree of perfection. —FATHER FRANCIS REMLER

Saint Frances Xavier Cabrini, pray for us.

. . . .

November 14

When it is all over, you will not regret having suffered; rather you will regret having suffered so little and suffered that little so badly. —BLESSED SEBASTIAN VALFRE

Saint Lawrence O'Toole, pray for us.

. . . .

November 15

When tempted, invoke your angel. He is more eager to help you than you are to be helped! Ignore the devil and do not be afraid of him; he trembles and flees at the sight of your guardian angel. —SAINT JOHN BOSCO

Saint Albert the Great, pray for us.

. . . .

. . . .

November 16

[W]hen night comes, and you look back over the day and
see how fragmentary everything has been, and how much
you planned that has gone undone, and all the reasons you
have to be embarrassed and ashamed: just take everything
exactly as it is, put it in God's hands and leave it with Him.
Then you will be able to rest in Him—really rest—and
start the next day as a new life.

—SAINT TERESA BENEDICTA OF THE CROSS

Saint Gertrude the Great, pray for us.

. . . .

November 17

[Modesty is] a ministry of beauty. —DAWN EDEN

Saint Elizabeth of Hungary, pray for us.

. . . .

November 18

My love for him is so strong that I don't want to
compromise his dignity. I intend to become his wife!

—FEMALE COLLEGE STUDENT

Saint Rose Philippine Duchesne, pray for us.

. . . .

. . . .

November 19

If then you are tempted to sin, reflect whether you have voluntarily brought it on yourself; and when the temptation is in itself sinful, whether you have cast yourself into it; that is, whether you might not have avoided the occasion, or have foreseen the temptation. If you have in no way induced it, then it cannot be imputed to you as sin.

—SAINT FRANCIS DE SALES

Saint Barlaam, pray for us.

. . . .

November 20

Purity of heart, like every virtue, calls for daily training of the will and constant interior discipline. It requires, above all, assiduous recourse to God in prayer. —POPE JOHN PAUL II

Saint Bernward, pray for us.

. . . .

November 21

To resist every temptation, it is sufficient to pronounce the names of Jesus and Mary; and if the temptation continues, let us continue to invoke Jesus and Mary, and the Devil shall never be able to conquer us.—SAINT ALPHONSUS LIGUORI

Holy Mary most pure, pray for us.

. . . .

. . . .

November 22

Lust is a poor, weak, whimpering whispering thing
compared with that richness and energy of desire which
will arise when lust has been killed. —C.S. LEWIS

Saint Cecilia, pray for us.

. . . .

November 23

All the sins of your life seem to be rising up against you.
Don't give up hope! On the contrary, call your holy mother
Mary, with the faith and abandonment of a child. She will
bring peace to your soul. —SAINT JOSEMARÍA ESCRIVÁ

Blessed Miguel Agustín Pro, pray for us.

. . . .

November 24

[P]ornography...seeks to foster precisely those distortions
of our sexual desires that we must struggle *against* in order
to discover true love. —CHRISTOPHER WEST

Saints Flora and Mary of Cordoba, pray for us.

. . . .

.   .   .   .

November 25

Love God more than me. —HIGH SCHOOL FEMALE

Blessed María Corsini, pray for us.

.   .   .   .

November 26

Love to be real, it must cost—it must hurt—it must empty us of self. —BLESSED TERESA OF CALCUTTA

Saint Leonard of Port Maurice, pray for us.

.   .   .   .

November 27

Carry the rosary with you everywhere, and it will carry you through anything. —JASON EVERT

Our Lady of the Miraculous Medal, pray for us.

.   .   .   .

．　．　．　．　．　．　．　．　．　．　．　．　．

November 28

Nothing can be more dangerous than keeping wicked companions. They communicate the infection of their vices to all who associate with them.

—SAINT JEAN BAPTISTE DE LA SALLE

Saint James of the Marches, pray for us.

．　．　．　．　．　．　．　．　．　．　．　．　．

November 29

You'd be surprised what guys are capable of when a girl has enough of a backbone to expect to be treated with dignity.

—CRYSTALINA EVERT

Saint Saturninus, pray for us.

．　．　．　．　．　．　．　．　．　．　．　．　．

November 30

One gift, one man. —HIGH SCHOOL FEMALE

Saint Andrew, pray for us.

．　．　．　．　．　．　．　．　．　．　．　．　．

DECEMBER

. . . .

December 1

Be a gentleman, like Jesus. —HIGH SCHOOL FEMALE

Saint Florentius, pray for us.

. . . .

December 2

Our sins are nothing but a grain of sand alongside the great
mountain of the mercy of God. —SAINT JOHN VIANNEY

Saint Bibiana, pray for us.

. . . .

December 3

Do not think that you are worthless or worth less because
of the past. No matter what has happened, you still have
yourself to give. —CRYSTALINA EVERT

Saint Francis Xavier, pray for us.

. . . .

. . . .

December 4

Filthy talk makes us feel comfortable with filthy action. But the one who knows how to control the tongue is prepared to resist the attacks of lust.

—SAINT CLEMENT OF ALEXANDRIA

Saint John Damascene, pray for us.

. . . .

December 5

Nothing in heaven compares to the beauty of God, and nothing on earth approaches the beauty of the woman. For this reason, women have a unique role in revealing God to the world. —JASON EVERT

Saint Gerald, pray for us.

. . . .

December 6

[D]o not accept anything as the truth if it lacks love. And do not accept anything as love which lacks truth!

—SISTER TERESA BENEDICTA OF THE CROSS

Saint Nicholas, pray for us.

. . . .

. . . .

December 7

We avoid the eyes of men to commit sin, yet we do it in God's presence. —SAINT AMBROSE

Saint Ambrose, pray for us.

. . . .

December 8

Our Lady's purity was not snow but fire. It was the kindling purity of white heat, and not the chilling purity of white cold.—FATHER VINCENT MCNABB

Immaculate Mary, pray for us.

. . . .

December 9

Girls like it when one of their dates is going to Mass.
—HIGH SCHOOL FEMALE

Saint Juan Diego, pray for us.

. . . .

. . . .

December 10
For a day in your courts is better
than a thousand elsewhere.
I would rather be a doorkeeper in the house of my God
than dwell in the tents of wickedness.
—PSALM 84:10

Pope Saint Gregory III, pray for us.

. . . .

December 11
[O]nly the chaste man and the chaste woman are capable
of true love. —POPE JOHN PAUL II

Pope Saint Damasus I, pray for us.

. . . .

. . . .

December 12

So your strength is failing you? Why don't you tell your
Mother about it?…

Mother! Call her with a loud voice. She is listening to you;
she sees you in danger, perhaps, and she—your holy mother
Mary—offers you, along with the grace of her Son, the
refuge of her arms, the tenderness of her embrace …
and you will find yourself with added strength for the
new battle. —SAINT JOSEMARÍA ESCRIVÁ

Our Lady of Guadalupe, pray for us.

. . . .

December 13

Remaining chaste in a relationship makes it so simple and
beautiful. It's like reliving the feeling of a first kiss, without
the weight of impurity haunting you. It's a beautiful thing.
—FEMALE COLLEGE STUDENT

Saint Lucy, pray for us.

. . . .

. . . .

December 14

Jesus says to each man, "Look at a crucifix. This is how I got my bride to heaven. How else do you think you will get yours there?" —JASON EVERT

Saint John of the Cross, pray for us.

. . . .

December 15

Joy is not a substitute for sex; sex is very often a substitute for Joy. —C.S. LEWIS

Saint Virginia Centurione Bracelli, pray for us.

. . . .

December 16

[E]very sin brings with it its own punishment. Apart from the possibility of serious infections, lewd people will never taste the true beauty of a sexual union based on mutual love and lived in reverence.

… [T]hey will experience lust, but their punishment is that they will never taste the sweetness of true love.

—DR. ALICE VON HILDEBRAND

Saint Adelaide, pray for us.

. . . .

· · · · · · · · · · · · ·

December 17

In high school we made fun of virgins in public, but I secretly respected and admired them, wishing I was in their place. At any point they could become like me, but I could never regain what they had. —CRYSTALINA EVERT

Saint Wivina, pray for us.

· · · · · · · · · · · · ·

December 18

[God] loves you, but even more—He longs for you. He misses you when you don't come close. He thirsts for you. He loves you always, even when you don't feel worthy. When not accepted by others, even by yourself sometimes—He is the one who always accepts you.... Only believe—you are precious to Him. Bring all you are suffering to His feet—only open your heart to be loved by Him as you are. He will do the rest.
—BLESSED TERESA OF CALCUTTA

Saint Gatian, pray for us.

· · · · · · · · · · · · ·

. . . .

December 19

The more you cling to Jesus the more capable you will become of being close to one another. —POPE JOHN PAUL II

Blessed Pope Urban V, pray for us.

. . . .

December 20

[One who has the habit of unclean speech is a] person whose lips are but an opening and a supply pipe which hell uses to vomit its impurities upon the earth.
—SAINT JOHN VIANNEY

Saint Theophilus, pray for us.

. . . .

December 21

By being pure, you're loving your body, you're loving your future children, you're loving your future spouse, and most importantly, you're loving your God. —CRYSTALINA EVERT

Saint Peter Canisius, pray for us.

. . . .

. . . .

December 22

Respect is the key to a girl's heart.

—HIGH SCHOOL FEMALE

Saints Chaeremon and Ishyrion, pray for us.

. . . .

December 23

Purity unites lovers in a foretaste of heaven, because they begin to see in each other a reflection of the face of God.

—JASON EVERT

Saint John of Kanty, pray for us.

. . . .

December 24

We can afford to lose castles, but we cannot let a day go by without attending holy Mass. —SAINT CHARLES OF BLOIS

Saint Charbel, pray for us.

. . . .

· · · · · · · · · · · · ·

December 25

The Eucharist is the secret of my day. It gives strength and meaning to all my activities of service to the Church and to the whole world....

Let Jesus in the Blessed Sacrament speak to your hearts. It is He who is the true answer of life that you seek.

He stays here with us: He is God with us. Seek Him without tiring, welcome Him without reserve, love Him without interruption: today, tomorrow, for ever!

—POPE JOHN PAUL II

Saint Mary and Saint Joseph, pray for us

· · · · · · · · · · · · ·

December 26

[I]n all these things we conquer overwhelmingly through him who loved us. —ROMANS 8:37, *NAB*

Saint Stephen, pray for us.

· · · · · · · · · · · · ·

· · · · · · · · · · · · · ·

December 27

Knowledge of your weakness is your greatest strength.
—Jason Evert

Saint John the Apostle, pray for us.

· · · · · · · · · · · · · ·

December 28

And what is the secret of perseverance? Love. Fall in Love,
and you will not leave him. —Saint Josemaría Escrivá

Holy Innocents, pray for us.

· · · · · · · · · · · · · ·

December 29

Silent lips are pure gold and bear witness to holiness
within. —Saint Faustina Kowalska

Saint Thomas à Becket, pray for us.

· · · · · · · · · · · · · ·

. . . .

December 30
Even as you seek a virtuous, fair, and good spouse,…
it is fitting that you should be the same.
—SAINT BERNARDINO OF SIENA

Holy Family, pray for us.

. . . .

December 31
When you decide firmly to lead a clean life, chastity will
not be a burden on you: it will be a crown of triumph.
—SAINT JOSEMARÍA ESCRIVÁ

Pope Saint Sylvester I, pray for us.

. . . .

INTRODUCTION

1. Josemaría Escrivá, *The Way* (New York: Scepter, 2002), p. 19. Copyright ©Studium Foundation, Madrid, Spain.

JANUARY

January 1. Philip Neri, as quoted in Stefano Manelli, *Jesus, Our Eucharistic Love* (Brookings, S.D.: Our Lady of Victory Mission, 1973), pp. 59–60.

January 2. Elisabeth Elliot, *Passion and Purity: Learning to Bring Your Love Life Under Christ's Control* (Grand Rapids: Revell, 1984), p. 21.

January 3. Francis de Sales, *An Introduction to the Devout Life*, part 4, chap. 8 (Rockford, Ill.: Tan, 1994), p. 261.

January 4. Wendy Shalit, *Girls Gone Mild: Young Women Reclaim Self-Respect and Find It's Not Bad to Be Good* (New York: Random House, 2007), p. 105.

January 5. Karol Wojtyla, *The Way to Christ: Spiritual Exercises* (San Francisco: Harper, 1994), p. 55.

January 9. Ephraem, as quoted in Paul Thigpen, *A Dictionary of Quotes from the Saints* (Ann Arbor, Mich.: Charis, 2001), p. 228.

January 10. Mother Teresa, foreword to Johann Christoph Arnold, *A Plea for Purity: Sex, Marriage, and God* (Farmington, Pa.: Plough, 1996).

January 12. John of the Cross, as quoted in Thigpen, p. 186.

January 14. Henry Cloud and John Townsend, *Boundaries in Dating: Making Dating Work* (Grand Rapids: Zondervan, 2000), p. 252.

January 15. Anthony Mottola, *The Spiritual Exercises of Saint Ignatius* (New York: Doubleday, 1989), pp. 131–132.

January 16. Julian of Norwich, as quoted in Thigpen, p. 229.

January 18. Venerable Catherine McAuley, *The Little Book of Catherine of Dublin* (Dublin: A Little Book Company, 2005), p. 22.

January 19. John Paul II, "We Wish to See Jesus," Message of the Holy Father John Paul II to the Youth of the World on the Occasion of the Nineteenth World Youth Day, February 22, 2004, no. 5, available at: www.ewtn.com.

January 20. José Luis González-Balado, ed., *Mother Teresa: In My Own Words* (New York: Gramercy, 1996), p. 33.

January 24. Francis de Sales, as quoted in Rosemary Ellen Guiley, *The Quotable Saint* (New York: Checkmark, 2002), p. 272.

January 26. Dawn Eden, *The Thrill of the Chaste* (Nashville: W Publishing Group, 2006), p. 6.

January 28. Thomas Aquinas, *Summa Theologiae,* IIa–IIae, 35: 4, ad 2, in Thomas Gilby, trans., *St. Thomas Aquinas: Philosophical Texts* (Whitefish, Mont.: Kessinger, 2003), p. 275.

January 30. Pope Benedict XVI, as quoted in "Having Kids Sends a Message, Says Pope," available at: www.zenit.org.

January 31. John Bosco, as quoted in Thigpen, p. 187.

FEBRUARY

February 1. Maria Faustina Kowalska, *Divine Mercy in My Soul: The Diary of the Servant of God Sister M. Faustina Kowalska,* Notebook 3, no. 1213 (Stockbridge, Mass.: Marian, 1987), p. 437.

February 3. John Paul II, *Mulieris Dignitatem,* Apostolic Letter on the Dignity and Vocation of Women, 14, available at: www.vatican.va.

February 5. Kowalska, p. 318.

February 6. Christopher West, *Good News About Sex and Marriage: Answers to Your Honest Questions About Catholic Teaching* (Ann Arbor, Mich.: Servant, 2000), p. 29.

February 7. Fulton Sheen, as quoted in *True Girl*, vol. 1, no. 1 (February/March 2006).

February 8. Escrivá, *The Way*, no. 118, p. 40.

February 12. C.S. Lewis, *The Four Loves* (New York: Harcourt, 1991), p. 121.

February 13. Pope John Paul II, address, April 29, 1989, Antananarivo, Madagascar, as quoted in Pedro Beteta López, ed., *The Meaning of Vocation (In the Words of John Paul II)* (Princeton, N.J.: Scepter, 1997), p. 28.

February 15. Eric and Leslie Ludy, *When God Writes Your Love Story* (Sisters, Oreg.: Loyal, 1999), p. 64.

February 17. Elliot, p. 145.

February 18. John Vianney, as quoted in Guiley, p. 274.

February 20. Francis of Assisi, A Letter to the Entire Order, in Regis J. Armstrong and Ignatius C. Brady, trans., *Francis and Clare: The Complete Works* (New York: Paulist, 1982), p. 58, as quoted in Sean Kinsella, "The Sacrament of Salt," *Adoremus Bulletin*, online edition, vol. 7, no. 6 (September 2001), available at: www.adoremus.org.

February 21. Lesley Walmsley, ed., *C.S Lewis on Love* (Nashville: Thomas Nelson, 1998), p. 28.

February 22. Escrivá, *The Way*, no. 755, p. 153.

February 24. Mother Teresa, as quoted in Arnold, foreword.

February 26. Karol Wojtyla, *Love and Responsibility*, H.T. Willets, trans. (San Francisco: Ignatius, 1993), p. 134.

MARCH

March 1. Josemaría Escrivá, *Furrow*, no. 836(New York: Scepter, 2002), p. 189.

March 2. G.K. Chesterton, *Orthodoxy* (New York: Doubleday, 1990), p. 57.

March 4. Cardinal John Henry Newman, *Discourses to Mixed Congregations*, "Purity and Love" (London: Longmans, Green, 1897), p. 4.

March 5. Henry Dieterich, ed., *Through the Year with Fulton Sheen: Inspirational Selections for Each Day of the Year* (San Francisco: Ignatius, 2003), pp. 194–195.

March 6. Pope John Paul II, Message to the Young People at the Kiel Center, St. Louis, January 26, 1999, no. 3, available at: www.usccb.org.

March 7. Jean C.J. d'Elbée, *I Believe in Love: A Personal Retreat Based on the Teaching of St. Thérèse of Lisieux* (Manchester, N.H.: Sophia Institute, 1974), p. 17.

March 8. Pope John Paul II, General Audience, November 24, 1982, in John Paul II, *Man and Woman He Created Them: A Theology of the Body* (Boston: Pauline, 2006), p. 519.

March 9. Dominic Savio, as quoted in Joseph Esper, *More Saintly Solutions to Life's Common Problems* (Manchester, N.H.: Sophia Institute, 2004), p. 186.

March 11. Josemaría Escrivá, *Christ Is Passing By* (New York: Scepter, 2002), p. 52.

March 15. Wojtyla, *Love and Responsibility*, p. 172.

March 16. Francis J. Remler, *How to Resist Temptation* (Manchester, N.H.: Sophia Institute, 2001), p. 103.

March 17. True Love Waits, "Interview with a Non-virgin," available at: www.lifeway.com.

March 18. Escrivá, *The Way*, no. 131, p. 41.

March 19. John Eldredge, *Wild at Heart: Discovering the Secret of a Man's Soul* (Nashville: Thomas Nelson, 2001), p. 62.

March 21. Elliot, pp. 185–186.

March 22. Sarah Hinlicky, "Subversive Virginity," *First Things*, October 1998, available at: www.firstthings.org.

March 23. Escrivá, *The Way*, no. 120, p. 40.

March 25. Basil the Great, as quoted in Guiley, p. 304.

March 28. Augustine, *On Christian Doctrine*, bk. 3, chap. 10, no. 16, in Philip Schaff, ed., *A Select Library of the Nicene and Post-Nicene Fathers of the Christian Church*, vol. 2, available at: www.ccel.org.

March 29. Francis de Sales, as quoted in Thigpen, p. 229.

March 30. John Climacus, *The Ladder of Divine Ascent,* "Step 3: On Exile or Pilgrimage" (Boston: Holy Transfiguration Monastery, 1978), quoted at www.innerlightproductions.com.

March 31. Escrivá, *Furrow,* no. 840, p. 189.

APRIL

April 2. John Paul II, *Redemptor Hominis,* 10, available at: www.vatican.va.

April 3. J. Budziszewski, "Designed for Sex: What We Lose When We Forget What Sex Is For," *Touchstone,* July/August 2005, available at: www.touchstonemag.com.

April 5. Peter of Alcantara, *Treatise on Prayer and Meditation,* as quoted in Guiley, p. 275.

April 7. John Vianney, "On the Sixth Commandment," in *Thoughts of the Curé d'Ars* (Rockford, Ill.: Tan, 1984), p. 63.

April 9. Pope John Paul II, as quoted in López, p. 22.

April 12. Augustine, *Confessions,* bk. 8, chap. 5, as quoted at lifeteen.com.

April 14. Laura Schlessinger, *Stupid Things Parents Do to Mess up Their Kids: Don't Have Them If You Won't Raise Them* (New York: Harper Collins, 2002), p. 167.

April 15. Escrivá, *The Way,* no. 121, p. 40.

April 16. Alice von Hildebrand, *The Privilege of Being a Woman* (Ann Arbor, Mich.: Veritas, 2002), p. 85.

April 19. T.G. Morrow, *Christian Courtship in an Oversexed World: A Guide for Catholics* (Huntington, Ind.: Our Sunday Visitor, 2003), p. 38.

April 21. Fulton J. Sheen, *Three to Get Married* (Princeton, N.J.: Scepter, 1951), pp. 80, 89.

April 23. Pope John Paul II, "We Wish to See Jesus," no. 2.

April 25. John Climacus, as quoted in Joseph M. Esper, *More Saintly Solutions to Life's Common Problems* (Manchester, N.H.: Sophia Institute, 2004), p. 188.

April 27. Alphonsus Liguori, *The Dignity and Duties of the Priest*, pt. 1, chap. 6, 3:1, available at: www.catholictradition.org.

April 28. *Love Is a Choice: The Life of St. Gianna Molla* (San Francisco: Ignatius, 2005), DVD.

April 29. Saint Catherine of Siena, letter 368, as referenced in Pope John Paul II, Homily at the Closing of World Youth Day, no. 7, August 20, 2000, available at: www.vatican.va.

April 30. Francis de Sales, as quoted in Thigpen, p. 229.

MAY

May 1. John Henry Newman, *Discourses to Mixed Congregations*, Discourse 18, "On the Fitness of the Glories of Mary," available at: www.newmanreader.org.

May 2. Wojtyla, *Love and Responsibility*, p. 131.

May 3. Cloud and Townsend, p. 251.

May 6. Escrivá, *The Way*, no. 513, p. 108.

May 7. Alphonsus Liguori, as quoted in Francis Edward Nugent, *"Fairest Star of All": A Little Treasury of Mariology* (Paterson, N.J.: St. Anthony Guild, 1956), p. 23.

May 9. Escrivá, *The Way*, no. 514, p. 108.

May 11. Escrivá, *The Way*, no. 144, p. 43.

May 12. Wendy Shalit, *A Return to Modesty: Discovering the Lost Virtue* (New York: Touchstone, 1999), p. 212.

May 13. "The Premise and Promise of Fatima," part 2, available at: www.dailycatholic.com.

May 14. John-Paul Day, as quoted in Edward Marriott, "Men and Porn," *The Guardian*, November 8, 2003.

May 15. Escrivá, *Furrow*, no. 847, pp. 190–191.

SOURCES

May 18. Pope John Paul II, Address to Young People, September 23, 2001, no. 6, available at: www.vatican.va.

May 19. Escrivá, *The Way*, no. 493, p. 105.

May 24. Henry Ward Beecher, as quoted in Les and Leslie Parrott, *Saving Your Marriage Before It Starts* (Grand Rapids, Mich.: Zondervan, 1995), p. 41.

May 25. Christopher West, *The Love That Satisfies: Reflections on Eros and Agape* (West Chester, Pa.: Ascension, 2007), p. 63.

May 26. Philip Neri, as quoted in devotional reading for May 26, 2008, available at: www.ewtn.com.

May 27. Fulton Sheen, as quoted in Nugent, p. 18.

May 28. Escrivá, *Furrow*, no. 849, p. 191.

May 30. Prayer of Mother Teresa, The Path of Love Homepage, available at: http://home.comcast.net/~motherteresasite.

JUNE

June 1. Pope John Paul II, as quoted in López, pp. 19–20.

June 3. Paul M. Quay, *The Christian Meaning of Human Sexuality* (San Francisco: Ignatius, 1985), p. 106.

June 5. Escrivá, *Furrow*, no. 831, p. 188.

June 6. Pope John Paul II, in Greg Burke, ed., *An Invitation to Joy: Selections From the Writings and Speeches of His Holiness John Paul II* (New York: Simon and Schuster, 2000), p. 49.

June 8. Christopher West, *Heaven's Song: Sexual Love As It Was Meant to Be* (West Chester, Pa.: Ascension, 2008), p. 86.

June 9. Mother Teresa, as quoted at www.motherteresa.com and www.chastity.com.

June 11. Von Hildebrand, *The Privilege of Being a Woman*, p. 90.

June 14. Basil the Great, as quoted in Thigpen, p. 228.

June 16. Remler, p. 92.

June 17. Mike Mathews, "'Sexy' Fashions … What Do Men Think?" available at: www.Lovematters.com.

June 19. Clement Hofbauer, as quoted in Esper, p. 187.

June 20. Pope John Paul II, *Crossing the Threshold of Hope* (New York: Knopf, 2001), p. 121.

June 22. Escrivá, *The Way*, no. 4, p. 21.

June 24. Thomas More, as quoted in Thigpen, p. 232.

June 25. Mother Teresa, as quoted by the Missionaries of the Blessed Sacrament, available at: www.ACFP2000.com.

June 26. Escrivá, *The Way*, no. 122, p. 40.

June 27. Eden, p. 9.

June 29. "Padre Pio: A Living Crucifix," Geraldine Nolan, trans., flyer printed by Our Lady of Grace Capuchin Friary Editions, available at: www.padrepio.org.uk.

June 30. Christopher West, *Heaven's Song*, pp. 153–154.

JULY

July 1. Augustine, as quoted in Thigpen, p. 28.

July 4. Pier Giorgio Frassati, To the Catholic Youth of Pollone, Italy, 1923, as quoted at www.cyainregina.ca and www.omsoul.com.

July 7. Escrivá, *Furrow*, no. 691, p. 158.

July 8. Quote displayed at the Pier Giorgio exhibit, World Youth Day 2008, Sydney.

July 9. Jill Murray, *But I Love Him: Protecting Your Teen Daughter from Controlling, Abusive Dating Relationships* (New York: HarperCollins, 2001), p. 81.

July 10. Pope John Paul II, as quoted in López, p. 19.

July 11. Remler, p. 31.

July 12. Lewis, *The Four Loves*, p. 121.

July 15. Bonaventure, as quoted in Alphonsus Liguori, *The Glories of Mary* (New York: P.J. Kenedy, 1888), no. 164, available at: www.archive.org.

July 16. Eden, p. 148.

July 17. Wendy M. Wright, Péronne Marie Thibert and Joseph F. Power, *Francis de Sales, Jane de Chantal: Letters of Spiritual Direction* (Mahwah, N.J.: Paulist, 1988), p. 118.

July 20. Padre Pio, as quoted in Vincent Falco, *Saint Padre Pio of Pietrelcina, Italy* (Miami: Falco, 2006), p. 14.

July 21. John Paul II, homily, "The Love Within Families," *Origins*, April 23, 1987, 799, as quoted in West, *Good News About Sex and Marriage*, p. 65.

July 22. Vatican II, The Council's Message to Women, December 8, 1965, as quoted in Pope John Paul II, *Mulieris Dignitatem*, 1, available at: www.vatican.va.

July 23. Escrivá, *The Forge* (New York: Scepter, 2002), no. 1055, p. 225.

July 25. Pope John Paul II, as quoted in López, pp. 18–19.

July 29. Pope John Paul II, Message for 2004 World Youth Day, Vatican City, March 1, 2004, available at: www.franciscanyouthusa.com.

July 30. Morrow, p. 106.

July 31. *Spiritual Exercises of St. Ignatius*, p. 132.

AUGUST

August 1. Alphonsus Liguori, *The True Spouse of Jesus Christ*, p. 413, as quoted in Rev. William A. Kaschmitter, *The Spirituality of the Catholic Church* (Houston, Tex.: Lumen Christi, 1982), p. 429.

August 3. Von Hildebrand, *The Privilege of Being a Woman*, p. 91.

August 4. *Thoughts of the Curé d'Ars*, p. 25.

August 6. Escrivá, *The Way*, no. 236, p. 59.

August 9. Edith Stein, *Essays on Woman*, as quoted in Guiley, p. 170.

August 10. Francis of Assisi, as quoted in Thigpen, p. 123.

August 11. Camille De Blasi, *Modestly Yours* (Snohomish, Wash.: Healing the Culture, 2004), p. 16.

August 12. Alphonsus Liguori, as quoted in Kaschmitter, p. 426.

August 14. Maximilian Kolbe, The Original Charter of the Militia Immaculatae, www.ewtn.com.

August 15. Fulton Sheen, *The World's First Love* (San Francisco: Ignatius, 1996), p. 20.

August 16. Saint John Chrysostom, *Homily 46 on the Gospel of John*, as quoted in Alphonsus Liguori, Sermon 31, Nicholas Callan, trans., *Sermons for All the Sundays in the Year* (Dublin: James Duffy and Sons, 1882).

August 19. Karol Wojtyla, *The Way to Christ*, p. 38.

August 20. Escrivá, *The Way*, no. 143, p. 43.

August 21. C.S. Lewis, *Mere Christianity*, as quoted in Lesley Walmsley, ed., *C.S. Lewis on Love* (Nashville: Thomas Nelson, 1998), p. 29.

August 22. Pope John Paul II, as quoted in López, p. 33.

August 23. West, *The Love That Satisfies*, p. 79.

August 24. Bruce Marshall, *The World, The Flesh, and Father Smith* (Boston: Houghton Mifflin, 1945), p. 108, as quoted at http://chesterton.org.

August 25. John Paul II, General Audience of April 1, 1981, in *The Theology of the Body: Human Love in the Divine Plan* (Boston: Pauline, 1997), pp. 213–214.

August 26. Sheen, *Three to Get Married*, p. 1.

August 27. Elliot, p. 131.

August 28. Philippe Lefebvre, as quoted in "Man-Woman Relationship, a Good Thing in Need of Healing," Interview With Biblical Exegete Anne-Marie Pelletier, March 9, 2005, Catholic Online, available at: www.catholic.org.

August 31. John Paul II, *Crossing the Threshold of Hope*, p. 123.

SOURCES

SEPTEMBER

September 1. Padre Pio, in Falco, p. 4.

September 2. John Paul II, General Audience May 30, 1984, as quoted in *Man and Woman He Created Them*, p. 572.

September 3. West, *Heaven's Song*, p. 47.

September 5. Michael Collopy, *Works of Love Are Works of Peace: Mother Teresa of Calcutta and the Missionaries of Charity* (San Francisco: Ignatius, 1996), p. 53.

September 6. Eden, 77.

September 7. Jill Haak Adels, *The Wisdom of the Saints* (New York: Oxford University Press, 1987), p. 59.

September 8. John Vianney, *Sermon on Purity*, in *Thoughts of the Curé d'Ars*, p. 73.

September 11. Pope John Paul II, Homily, Seventeenth World Youth Day, Toronto, July 28, 2002, no. 5, available at: www.vatican.va.

September 14. John Vianney, "The Armed Crosses," in Una Morrissy, trans., *The Sermons of the Curé of Ars* (Rockford, Ill.: Tan, 1995), pp. 180–181.

September 16. Wojtyla, *Love and Responsibility*, p. 169.

September 17. Robert Bellarmine, *The Art of Dying Well*, as quoted in Guiley, p. 135.

September 18. Escrivá, *The Way*, as quoted in Guiley, p. 8.

September 20. Eden, p. xii.

September 23. Padre Pio, Letter, 1920, as quoted in Guiley, p. 273.

September 24. Arnold, p. 39.

September 25. John Paul II, *The Theology of the Body*, p. 376.

September 26. Sheen, *Three to Get Married*, p. 85.

September 28. Address by a Vacationing John Paul II, Les Combes, Italy, July 11, 2004, available at: www.zenit.org.

September 29. Kowalska, *Divine Mercy in My Soul*, as quoted in Guiley, p. 5.

September 30. Jerome, *Letter to Furia*, no. 7, in Philip Schaff, ed., *The Principal Works of St. Jerome*, in *Nicene and Post-Nicene Fathers*, second series, vol. 6, available at: www.ccel.org.

OCTOBER

October 1. Thérèse of Lisieux, as quoted in Joe Hanley and Jack Manhire, eds., *Classic Quotes of Catholic Spirituality* (Chicago: PLS, n.d.), p. 9.

October 2. John Vianney, *On Temptation*, as quoted in *Thoughts of the Curé d'Ars*, p. 59.

October 3. Eden, p. 22.

October 4. Thomas of Celano, *The First Life of Saint Francis of Assisi*, chap. 83, as quoted in "Words of St. Francis: Temptations and Tribulations," available at: www.secularfranciscans.org.

October 5. Kowalska, p. 63.

October 7. Escrivá, *The Way*, no. 558, p. 117.

October 8. Shalit, *A Return to Modesty*, p. 157.

October 10. Pope John Paul II, Address at Close of Centenary Year of the death of Saint Maria Goretti, quoted in "Chastity Safeguards Love, Says John Paul II," Vatican City, July 6, 2003, available at: www.zenit.org.

October 13. "Premise and Promise of Fatima."

October 15. Teresa of Avila, as quoted in Thigpen, p. 199.

October 16. Von Hildebrand, *The Privilege of Being a Woman,* p. 63.

October 18. Pope John Paul II, Address of January 13, 1996, Manila, as quoted in López, p. 23.

October 20. Morrow, p. 43.

October 21. Escrivá, *Furrow*, no. 475, p. 114.

October 23. Arnold, p. 41.

October 24. Dietrich von Hildebrand, *Purity: The Mystery of Christian Sexuality* (Steubenville, Ohio: Franciscan University Press, 1989), pp. 40–41.

October 25. Escrivá, *The Way*, no. 983, p. 197.

October 26. Benjamin Tillett, as quoted in Parrott, p. 68.

October 28. Shalit, *A Return to Modesty*, p. 102.

October 31. Escrivá, *Furrow*, no. 478, p. 115.

November

November 1. Pope Clement I, quoted in Thigpen, p. 198.

November 4. Wojtyla, *Love and Responsibility*, p. 208.

November 5. Søren Kierkegaard, *Either-Or* (written under the pseudonym of Victor Eremita) (Princeton, N.J.: Princeton University Press, 1946), p. 56.

November 6. Augustine, as quoted in Thigpen, p. 43.

November 8. Jerome, Letter 384, as quoted in Guiley, p. 154.

November 9. Sheen, *Three to Get Married*, p. 81.

November 11. John Vianney, as quoted in Guiley, p. 274.

November 13. Remler, p. 92.

November 14. Sebastian Valfre, as quoted in Haak Adels, p. 64.

November 15. John Bosco, as quoted in Thigpen, p. 15.

November 16. Teresa Benedicta of the Cross, as quoted in "Edith Stein" available at: www.ewtn.com.

November 17. Eden, p. 150.

November 19. Francis de Sales, as quoted in Guiley, p. 272.

November 20. Pope John Paul II, Address at the Conclusion of the Centenary of the Death of St. Maria Goretti, www.zenit.org.

November 21. Alphonsus Liguori, as quoted in Guiley, p. 273.

November 22. C.S. Lewis, *The Great Divorce* (New York: HarperCollins, 2001), p. 102.

November 23. Escrivá, *The Way*, no. 498, p. 106.

November 24. West, *Good News About Sex and Marriage*, p. 84.

November 26. Mother Teresa, as quoted in Collopy, p. 30.

November 28. Jean Baptiste de la Salle, as quoted in Thigpen, p. 20.

DECEMBER

December 2. John Vianney, as quoted in Thigpen, p. 150

December 4. Clement of Alexandria, *The Teacher,* as quoted in Guiley, p. 163.

December 6. Teresa Benedicta of the Cross, as quoted in Homily of John Paul II for the Canonization of Edith Stein, October 11, 1998, available at: www.vatican.va.

December 7. Ambrose of Milan, as quoted in Thigpen, p. 212.

December 8. Vincent McNabb, as quoted in Nugent, no. 117, p. 29.

December 11. Wojtyla, *Love and Responsibility*, p. 171.

December 12. Escrivá, *The Way*, nos. 515, 516, p. 108.

December 15. C.S. Lewis, *Surprised by Joy: The Shape of My Early Life* (New York: Harcourt, Brace & World, 1955), p. 170.

December 16. Von Hildebrand, *The Privilege of Being a Woman*, p. 95.

December 18. Mother Teresa, "I Thirst," March 25, 1993, as quoted in Collopy, p. 197.

December 19. Pope John Paul II, Message to the Youth of the World on the Occasion of the Twelfth World Youth Day, August 15, 1996, no. 5, available at: www.vatican.va.

December 20. John Vianney, as quoted in Guiley, p. 226.

December 24. Charles of Blois, as quoted in Thigpen, p. 40.

December 25. Pope John Paul II, "The Eucharist Is the Secret of My Day," *L'Osservatore Romano*, October 8, 1997, p. 7.

December 28. Escrivá, *The Way*, no. 999, p. 199.

December 29. Kowalska, p. 234.

December 30. Bernardino of Siena, as quoted in Thigpen, p. 140.

December 31. Escrivá, *The Way*, no. 123, p. 40.

PURITY 365